14 $\frac{\times 2-19}{2-20}$

Francis Crick and
James Watson

And the Building Blocks of Life

Owen Gingerich
General Editor

Francis Crick and James Watson

And the Building Blocks of Life

Edward Edelson

Oxford University Press
New York • Oxford

Fondly dedicated to Hannah, the newest member of the family.

Oxford University Press

Oxford New York
Athens Auckland Bangkok Bogotá Bombay
Buenos Aires Calcutta Cape Town Dar es Salaam
Delhi Florence Hong Kong Istanbul Karachi
Kuala Lumpur Madras Madrid Melbourne
Mexico City Nairobi Paris Singapore
Taipei Tokyo Toronto Warsaw
and associated companies in
Berlin Ibadan

Design: Design Oasis
Layout: Leonard Levitsky
Picture research: Lisa Kirchner

Library of Congress Cataloging-in-Publication Data

Edelson, Edward
James Watson and Francis Crick and the building blocks of life / Edward Edelson.
p. c. — (Oxford portraits in science)
Includes bibliographical references and index.
ISBN 0-19-511451-5 (library edition)
1. Watson, James D., 1928– —Juvenile literature. 2. Crick, Francis, 1916–
—Juvenile literature. 3. DNA—Research—Juvenile literature. 4. Molecular biolo-
gists—Biography—Juvenile literature. [1.Watson, James D., 1928– . 2. Crick,
Francis, 1916– . 3. Molecular biologists. 4. DNA—Research.] I. Title. II. Series.
QP624.E34   1998
572.8'6'072—dc21   97-42791
                     CIP
                     AC

9 8 7 6 5 4 3 2 1

Printed in the United States of America
on acid-free paper

On the cover: *Francis Crick and James Watson in 1993;* Inset: *Watson and Crick in 1953.*

Frontispiece: *Watson and Francis at the Cavendish Laboratory at Cambridge University in 1953.*

Contents

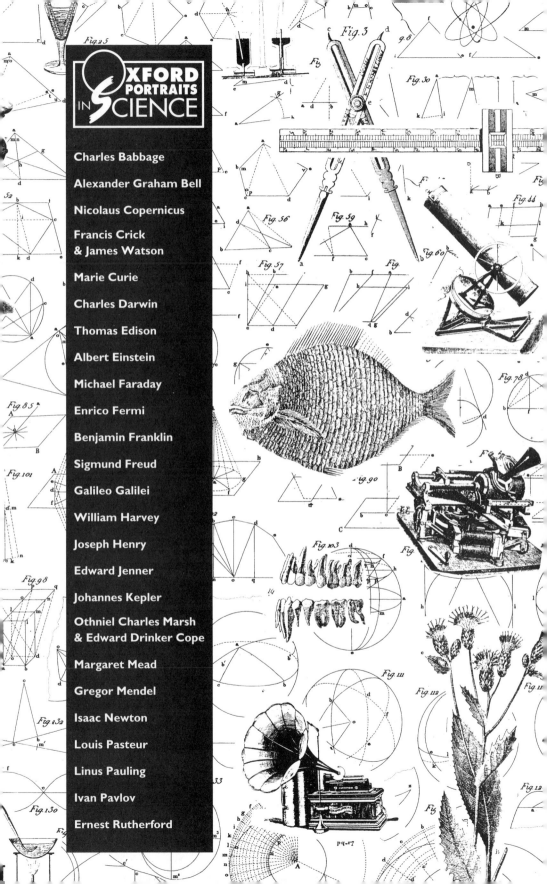

OXFORD PORTRAITS IN SCIENCE

A Story of Two Men and a New Science

This is an unusual biography, in several ways. First, it is the biography of two people, not one. The names of James Watson and Francis Crick are bound together forever. You cannot mention Watson without mentioning Crick, because the discovery they made about the molecule of life was truly a joint enterprise. (Years after the discovery, Crick recalled introducing Watson to someone at the laboratory where Crick was working. "Watson?" the person said in surprise. "I thought your name was Watson-Crick.")

This story is also unusual because the heart of their narrative and the discovery they achieved covers just a few years rather than a lifetime. After that achievement, they went on to do distinguished work separately and rarely worked together again. But it is the one finding that they reported in 1953 that put their names indelibly in the history book of science. What they discovered was the secret of life, in molecular form. They were the first to describe the structure of deoxyribonucleic acid, DNA, the molecule that carries the information of life.

An information-carrying segment of DNA is called a gene. Genes determine the basic nature of all living things,

Francis Crick and James Watson in 1993, at the 40th anniversary celebration of the publication of their historic Nature *magazine article, in which they described the molecular structure of DNA for the first time.*

including humans, and so DNA is considered the most important molecule of life. Specifically, genes carry the information for the production of proteins, the molecules that make up most of the body. When Watson and Crick described the structure of DNA, they thus opened the door to a new science of genetics—and, beyond that, the science of molecular biology—a field that is still growing and developing, and one that is having an increasing influence on medicine and on all of biology.

The names and work of many other scientists are an essential part of this story. Some of those scientists set the stage for what Watson and Crick accomplished. Some were competitors in a race to accomplish what Watson and Crick were the first to achieve. Others joined Watson and Crick to build on the DNA discovery—first to decode the genetic message carried in that molecule, then to show how information is transferred from DNA (correctly or incorrectly) to govern the production of proteins and thus to shape living things. And since this is a story of modern science, the actors in it were from a number of countries and moved around frequently, attending a variety of meetings and moving from one laboratory to another, and often from country to country.

Finally, the full consequences of what Watson and Crick discovered are still being explored. Theirs is a story that began more than 40 years ago, is still being told, and has implications that will extend well into the 21st century.

One example of this ongoing effort is the Human Genome Project, a program to make a map of the entire human genetic apparatus, called the genome; to identify all the genes that make us what we are; and to find the complete sequence of subunits within the genome. In addition to its basic scientific value, this information can be used to detect and help treat young people and unborn children with inherited genetic diseases. It can also identify adults at high risk of diseases such as breast cancer, in which individual genes play a role—an effort that has already begun. Watson helped the Human Genome Project get off to a good start, serving as its director during the critical early years.

Researchers building on the work done by Watson and Crick have established the technique in which genes can be manipulated and transferred. Recombinant DNA technology has become both a new industry and a new medical field. Proteins used in medicine, such as insulin and human growth hormone, are produced by genetic engineering—the process of putting the appropriate genes into corresponding bacteria, which then turn out large amounts of the medicinal protein. The same genetic technology is also being used in agriculture, to develop species of plants that are resistant to attack by insects and other predators, to increase production of milk and crops, and to make flowers with new colors and patterns. And now it has even become possible to clone mammals and other animals, creating exact genetic copies of individual animals by transferring DNA from one cell to another.

Genetic technology is also being used in medicine, to treat genetic diseases by giving patients normal genes to replace flawed genes causing serious problems. The first attempt at human gene therapy took place in 1990. Researchers at a National Institutes of Health facility treated a young girl with a deficiency in her immune system that prevented her from responding normally to fight off infectious agents such as disease-causing bacteria. They gave her 1 billion immune system cells that had been genetically engineered to provide the protection she lacked. A number of other gene therapy trials have been made since then, and the field is growing.

The subject of all this work is the cell, the smallest unit of living things. The body is made up of billions of cells, each with a specialized purpose. A brain cell is different from a skin cell, which is different from a muscle cell, and so on. Cells are very small, invisible to the naked eye. A sin-

The first X-ray diffraction photograph of a stretched, dried film of DNA. X-ray diffraction photos were used to determine the three-dimensional structure of biological molecules.

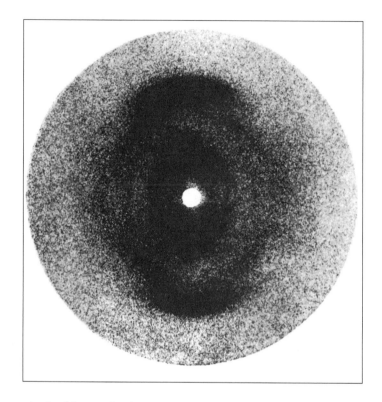

gle freckle on the back of your hand, for example, contains several thousand cells.

Under a high-powered microscope, cells show two kinds of basic internal structure. Most of the cells in the human body, for example, consist mainly of a large segment called the cytoplasm, at the center of which is a small unit called a nucleus. It is the nucleus that contains DNA, the genetic material. Within the nucleus are chromosomes—furled, stringlike bodies that are made up of DNA and thus contain the genes. The nucleus also holds the cellular machinery for activating the information contained in the genes and for reproducing the chromosomes. If you could take all the chromosomes out of one cell and unfurl them, they would stretch about six feet in length. Somewhere in those six feet would be between 50,000 and 100,000 genes, separated by long segments of DNA having no apparent purpose.

Cells whose chromosomes are in a nucleus are called eukaryotic cells. Complex organisms such as animals and most plants are eukaryotic. Bacteria and algae contain DNA, but they do not have a nucleus and are therefore called prokaryotic cells. The simpler organisms called viruses, which cause diseases like the common cold, also contain DNA or a closely related molecule, RNA (ribonucleic acid), but they have no cytoplasm and no internal mechanism for reproduction. A virus consists of a nucleic acid center inside a protein coat. Viruses reproduce by invading a living cell, seizing control of its reproductive apparatus, and killing the cell by having it turn out nothing but viruses.

Whether they are prokaryotic or eukaryotic, most cells reproduce themselves. (Some specialized cells, such as those in the brain and nervous system, eventually stop reproducing.) Cell metabolism and reproduction are complicated processes; more than 2,500 different molecules have been identified in even the simplest cells. Among the largest and most important of these molecules are the proteins and nucleic acids, both of which are made up of many connected subunits. DNA is the master molecule that ultimately governs the production of proteins and, through them, all the processes of cell metabolism and growth. Thus, knowing the structure of DNA and how it functions can truly be described as understanding the secret of life. That is what Crick and Watson discovered.

2

Dr. Watson Meets Mr. Crick

On April 25, 1953, the science journal *Nature* published a paper entitled "Molecular Structure of Nucleic Acids: A Structure for Deoxyribose Nucleic Acid." The paper was submitted by James D. Watson and Francis H. C. Crick. It was a short paper, just 128 lines in print, but it stands as a landmark in the history of science. Those few lines carried nothing less than the code of life on earth. Our lives and our health today are being shaped in many ways by the ramifications of that scientific paper.

When they published their paper, Watson and Crick were young scientists, not widely known at all. But that paper changed the situation totally. Suddenly they were among the most famous scientists in the world. In a few years of intensive effort they had won a high-stakes race against some of the most distinguished scientists in the United States and Europe.

The collaboration of Watson and Crick lasted only a few years before their careers moved in different directions, yet their achievement was enough to tie their names together forever in the history of science. And it also established a firm footing for a branch of science that was just

MOLECULAR STRUCTURE OF NUCLEIC ACIDS

A Structure for Deoxyribose Nucleic Acid

This landmark article by Watson and Crick, published in Nature *magazine on April 25, 1953, revealed the molecular structure of DNA—the code of life on earth.*

WE wish to suggest a structure for the salt of deoxyribose nucleic acid (D.N.A.). This structure has novel features which are of considerable biological interest.

A structure for nucleic acid has already been proposed by Pauling and Corey[1]. They kindly made their manuscript available to us in advance of publication. Their model consists of three intertwined chains, with the phosphates near the fibre axis, and the bases on the outside. In our opinion, this structure is unsatisfactory for two reasons: (1) We believe that the material which gives the X-ray diagrams is the salt, not the free acid. Without the acidic hydrogen atoms it is not clear what forces would hold the structure together, especially as the negatively charged phosphates near the axis will repel each other. (2) Some of the van der Waals distances appear to be too small.

Another three-chain structure has also been suggested by Fraser (in the press). In his model the phosphates are on the outside and the bases on the inside, linked together by hydrogen bonds. This structure as described is rather ill-defined, and for this reason we shall not comment on it.

We wish to put forward a radically different structure for the salt of deoxyribose nucleic acid. This structure has two helical chains each coiled round the same axis (see diagram). We have made the usual chemical assumptions, namely, that each chain consists of phosphate di-ester groups joining β-D-deoxyribofuranose residues with 3',5' linkages. The two chains (but not their bases) are related by a dyad perpendicular to the fibre axis. Both chains follow right-handed helices, but owing to the dyad the sequences of the atoms in the two chains run in opposite directions. Each chain loosely resembles Furberg's[2] model No. 1; that is, the bases are on the inside of the helix and the phosphates on the outside. The configuration of the sugar and the atoms near it is close to Furberg's 'standard configuration', the sugar being roughly perpendicular to the attached base. There is a residue on each chain every 3·4 A. in the z-direction. We have assumed an angle of 36° between adjacent residues in the same

then emerging: molecular biology, the study of the structure and function of the molecules that govern the development and activities of living things.

The creation of the idea of molecular biology was the newest step in a drastic change in the scientific conception of living things. This change had come about perhaps a century earlier, when the detailed scientific study of living things had begun in earnest. At that time, many people drew a rigid line between inanimate objects and living creatures. Their idea was that living things were too complex to be explained by the rules of science that applied to ordinary objects.

Molecular biology did away with the last vestiges of that belief. Its guiding principle was—and is—that most, if not all, of the characteristics of living beings can be explained by studying the molecules of which they are made. At the center of molecular biology is deoxyribonucleic acid, DNA, the molecule whose composition determines almost all of those characteristics. The work by Watson and Crick was a milestone in establishing the importance of molecular biology.

Watson and Crick were not alone. They worked with, competed against, and drew upon the efforts of distinguished—and almost invariably older—scientists in a number of countries. From the start, they knew they were in a competition of world-class ranking. Emotions could run high in such a competition. Hatred, jealousy, and admiration were all displayed by different players at different times. It was far from certain that the eventual outcome of the story would center on Watson and Crick; a change or twist here and there would have made all the difference. Yet it was this team that won in the end.

It was a day early in October 1951 when a young American scientist named James Dewey Watson met an older British scientist named Francis Harry Compton Crick at the Cavendish Laboratory of Cambridge University in England. At first glance, the two men appeared to have little or nothing in common. They came from different backgrounds in different countries and had what seemed to be very different personalities.

Jim Watson, the American, appeared on the surface to be soft spoken and self-effacing, a quiet man on most occasions. (His brashness would emerge later, in the book he wrote about the hunt for the structure of DNA, *The Double Helix*.) He was also a strange-looking figure in the Britain of that time, tall and lanky and very American-looking to the British eye. One secretary at Cambridge described him as bald, because he had a crew cut, quite different from the longer hair of most British scientists. After he heard that description, Watson immediately began to let his hair grow.

Crick, in contrast to Watson, had a booming voice and was fond of talking ("I have never seen Francis Crick in a modest mood," Watson was to write years later as the opening sentence of *The Double Helix*). The two young men even came from different scientific disciplines. What they did have in common, however, was brilliance—which was to fashion a partnership that wrote a memorable chapter in the history of science.

Jim Watson was born in Chicago in 1928 into a family without much money. His father was a bill collector whose hobby was birdwatching, a pastime he taught to young Jim. His mother worked as a secretary at the University of Chicago. In his early years, Jim Watson carried on a running debate with his mother about the relative importance of nature—inheritance—versus nurture in shaping individuals. Watson used to argue the side of the environment, while his mother stressed the importance of heredity.

Young Jim Watson attended Chicago's public schools, where his intelligence was evident from the start. In those days there was a radio program called *Quiz Kids,* on which bright youngsters amazed the listeners by answering difficult questions demanding encyclopedic knowledge. Jim Watson was a Quiz Kid. But he lasted only three sessions before being let go, because he made mistakes on questions about Shakespeare and religion, two subjects that did not interest him much.

Being a bookish child did not make life easy for Watson. "I wasn't a popular kid," he recalled decades later.

"I suspect it was because I would generally say something which I thought was true. In those days, I used to think manners were terrible—the truth was important and manners often hid the truth."

In those days, the University of Chicago was run by an educator named Robert Hutchins who had the revolutionary idea of admitting bright students two years before they would have graduated from high school and allowing them to take a full four-year set of college courses. Jim Watson entered the University of Chicago in 1943, at the age of 15, helped somewhat by the fact that his mother worked for the university. Watson lived at home, taking the streetcar to his classes.

At that time, Watson's major interest was in birds, and he wanted to make a career in ornithology. He demonstrated his intelligence by graduating from the University of Chicago with a degree in biology in just three years, in 1946, but stayed on for another year. He spent the summer of 1946 at the University of Michigan taking a course in ornithology, but his interest in birds soon faded.

Watson applied to graduate school in biochemistry at Harvard—and was turned down. He applied to the California Institute of Technology, but was rejected again. Finally he was given a research fellowship for the 1947–48 academic year at Indiana University in Bloomington, with a stipend of $900 (enough to live on at the time).

Watson was an unusual-looking fellow at the university—tall, thin, awkward, always dressed casually, usually wearing tennis shoes, not able to make many friends. In the seminars that were held on Friday evenings so graduate students could discuss their work, he made some enemies by his habit of opening a book to read if he considered the speaker to be dull.

Because of Watson's obvious brilliance, and despite his bad manners, the university extended his financial support after his research fellowship ended. Watson earned his doctorate in biochemistry at Indiana in May 1950, then looked around for a place where he could continue his work. It was arranged for him to go to Europe. At the age of 21, he was granted a fellowship to work on biochemistry in Copenhagen.

But reading *What Is Life?,* a book by the great scientist Erwin Schrödinger, changed his outlook. Schrödinger said that the gene was the central issue in the study of biology

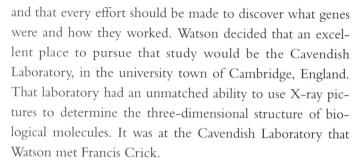

and that every effort should be made to discover what genes were and how they worked. Watson decided that an excellent place to pursue that study would be the Cavendish Laboratory, in the university town of Cambridge, England. That laboratory had an unmatched ability to use X-ray pictures to determine the three-dimensional structure of biological molecules. It was at the Cavendish Laboratory that Watson met Francis Crick.

Crick had also read Schrödinger's book. As he wrote later, it "conveyed in an exciting way the idea that, in biology, molecular explanations would not only be extremely important but also that they were just around the corner. This had been said before, but Schrödinger's book was very timely and attracted people who might otherwise not have entered biology at all."

As a boy, Francis Crick (here with his younger brother, left) worried that there would not be anything left for him to discover by the time he grew up and became a scientist.

Crick, like Watson, was born to parents who were not rich. They were shoe merchants in a town called Northampton, whose main business was shoe manufacturing (the local soccer team was called the Cobblers). Crick was born in 1916, which made him 12 years older than Watson.

Young Francis Crick went to a typical public school (as private schools are called in England). There he displayed an intense interest in science. That interest, he wrote many years later, came from reading a children's encyclopedia his parents bought for him. Its articles on sci-

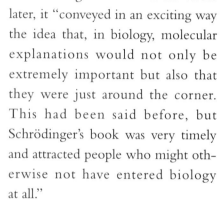

ence appealed to him most, especially stories of scientific discovery. He decided that he would be a scientist and discover things. "But I foresaw one snag," he wrote later. "By the time I grew up—and how far away that seemed—everything would have been discovered." His mother reassured him that there would be plenty left to find out.

By the time he was 10, Francis Crick was doing experiments at home. One of them was to put an explosive mixture into bottles and blow them up. His parents therefore imposed a rule that a bottle could be blown up only when it was in a pail of water, so that the pieces would not fly through the air.

Crick enrolled in University College, London, studying physics. Then as now, obtaining a doctorate in a scientific field was an essential step in establishing a career in that field. Crick had his master's degree and was close to obtaining his doctorate in physics when World War II broke out. That had an immediate, direct effect on his work. His laboratory was destroyed by a German bomb, and pursuing his academic studies became impossible.

During the war, Crick worked for the British Admiralty on underwater mines—how to make them, how to find them, how to destroy them. He came to Cambridge University after the war, in 1947, at age 31, still without a doctorate.

By then Crick's interests had shifted to biology. Applying for a student research grant, he wrote that "the particular field which excited my interest

Francis Crick as an undergraduate student in the late 1930s, outside his parents' house in Mill Hill, in North London.

is the division between the living and the non-living, as typified by, say, proteins, viruses, bacteria and the structure of chromosomes. The eventual goal, which is somewhat remote, is the description of these activities in terms of their structure. . . . This might be called the chemical physics of biology." Crick moved over to the Cavendish Laboratory, a part of Cambridge University, in 1949.

Crick later recalled how he met Watson. "I came home one day. We were living in a little flat in the center of Cambridge in those days, and my wife said to me, 'Oh Max was round here with a young American, and do you know, he had no hair.' [That crew cut again.] . . . I don't recall exactly the moment we met. I remember the chats we had over those first two or three days."

The apartment where Crick and his French-born wife, Odile, lived, was in the upper floor of a several-hundred-year-old house in Cambridge. It was very small, but as Watson later recalled, "despite the cramp, its great charm, magnified by Odile's decorative sense, gave it a cheerful, if not playful spirit."

Odile was Crick's second wife. His first marriage had not lasted long and a son, Michael, lived with Crick's mother. Odile was a free spirit and a good cook. She not only brightened Crick's life but also provided him with meals that were far superior to the standard British fare of tasteless meat, boiled potatoes, and colorless greens. Watson was soon eating dinner with them several nights a week.

One of Odile's charms, Watson later recalled, was that she wasn't offended by Crick's open admiration of young women who "showed some vitality and were distinctive in any way that permitted gossip and amusement." She also introduced Crick to a world of arts and crafts that was entirely new to him.

Words flowed freely when Crick, Odile, and Watson spent evenings together. One story that Watson remembered was of a costume party that Crick went to dressed as

George Bernard Shaw, the red-bearded author. As soon as Crick entered, he realized that it was a ghastly error, since not one of the young women enjoyed being tickled by the wet, scraggly hairs when he came within kissing distance.

Francis Crick with his son, Michael, in the early 1940s, when Crick was working for the British Admiralty on underwater mines.

Crick and Watson became friends as soon as they met. "Jim and I hit it off immediately, partly because our interests were astonishingly similar and partly, I suspect, because a certain youthful arrogance, a ruthlessness and an impatience with sloppy thinking came naturally to both of us," Crick wrote later in his autobiography. Soon they were having lunch almost every day in a picturesque pub, the Eagle, a block away from the Cavendish Laboratory, and talking almost nonstop at the laboratory. "We're going to put you and him in the same office and you can talk to each other and not disturb the rest of us," one senior scientist finally said to Crick.

As Crick wrote about Watson, "He was the first person I met who thought the same way about biology as I did. . . . I decided that genetics was the really essential part, what the genes were and what they did. And Watson was the first person I had met who had exactly the same ideas as I had. . . . Our ideas of a general nature were already formed when we met, and we merely, as it were, went on to discuss the details—what were genes made of and so on."

The two brought different kinds of expertise to the studies they wanted to do. Watson was trained in biology, the study of nature and the chemistry of living things. Crick had been trained in physics, which ordinarily does not deal with the nature of living things. He, too, had been made to change his attitude by reading Schrödinger's book *What Is Life?*

As Crick noted, their conversations began to center on the pressing biological issue of the day: determining the structure of the molecule that made up human genes, deoxyribonucleic acid, abbreviated as DNA. It was apparent to them and to numerous other scientists that finding the structure of DNA would answer many basic questions about living things and how they reproduce. Watson and Crick decided to use X rays to look at the structure of DNA.

For Crick, agreeing to study DNA was a major career change. He had been working on proteins for two years and was just beginning to master the subject. It would take at least two years to make the full switch to studying DNA. In addition, there was a personal problem. At that time, the study in England of the DNA molecule was dominated by Maurice Wilkins, a scientist at King's College in London who was using X-ray diffraction as his basic tool. Crick thus put himself in direct competition with Wilkins, an awkward situation in the small world of British science. Nonetheless, he did it.

In tackling the DNA issue with Watson, Crick later wrote, their personalities and positions meshed: "If I had some idea, which as it turned out was going off at a tangent, Watson would tell me in no uncertain terms this was nonsense, and vice versa. It is one of the requirements for collaboration of this sort that you must be perfectly candid, one might almost say rude, to the person you are working with. It is useless working with someone who is either much too junior than yourself, or much too senior, because then politeness creeps in, and this is the end of all good collaboration in science."

The Road to DNA

The thread leading to the question about DNA that Watson and Crick wanted to answer—its exact molecular structure—went back more than a century, to work done in obscurity by a German monk named Gregor Mendel.

Mendel was born early in the 18th century into a dirt-poor family in what is now Austria. His brightness was evident from the start, and he was able to gain entrance to a university. But his family was too poor to pay his tuition, and the resulting stress caused him to have a nervous breakdown. In 1843 he became a monk and entered a monastery near the city of Brno, a move that eliminated his financial problems and enabled him to pursue his intellectual studies. He was even able to spend two years at the University of Vienna, taking courses that strengthened his mathematical abilities.

When he returned to his monastery, Mendel began applying his mathematical knowledge to the study of inheritance. Other scientists had tried such studies but had abandoned them because of the complexity of the traits that can be passed from one generation to the next. Where others had failed, Mendel succeeded—fabulously. What he did in

German abbot Gregor Mendel is credited with discovering the basic rules of inheritance and modern genetics. Watson and Crick used Mendel's research as a foundation for their own work.

relatively few years was to establish the basic framework of modern genetics.

When Watson and Crick began to work on DNA, the field had long since acknowledged Mendel's work. He remained unknown only until 1899, when three scientists, Hugo de Vries in the Netherlands, Carl Correns in Germany, and Erich Tschermak von Seysenegg in Austria, were preparing to publish the results of research they had carried out that essentially repeated what Mendel had done. Looking through the scientific literature, they found the paper that Mendel had published years earlier. When they learned about this earlier work, they immediately gave Mendel credit for being the first to discover the basic rules of inheritance.

Then complications began to emerge. In England, William Bateson did experiments in which he crossed a strain of sweet peas that had purple flowers and long pollen grains with a strain having red flowers and round pollen grains. He found that in succeeding generations these traits were not usually inherited independently. More often, as he wrote, "There is evidence of a linking or coupling between distinct characters."

Other researchers working with other species and different traits also began to discover that many traits were not

The brothers of the Augustinian Monastery in Old Brno in the 1860s. Mendel is standing second from the right, holding a flower.

always inherited independently, and that two versions of a trait sometimes could blend to achieve a compromise result. As geneticists began to work with more and more complex organisms, they came to realize that a trait was not always the result of one gene alone, but sometimes of several genes working together.

It turned out that Mendel had been lucky in the plants and traits he had chosen to study, because they did not have linked inheritances. Had he chosen another species or another trait, the results might have been quite different. However, Mendel did establish the basic rules by which all the complexities of inheritance can be studied. Today this field is called Mendelian genetics.

The next question to be asked concerned inheritance in people: How are traits such as blond hair or blue eyes, or being short or tall, passed from generation to generation in humans? Jim Watson and Francis Crick supplied a key answer to this question, building on research that went back decades.

The general process of human birth was already known: a sperm from a man unites with an egg (formally, an ovum) from a woman to create a zygote, a single cell that has genetic material from both the father and the mother. This zygote begins to divide again and again, multiplying by 2, 4, 8, 16, 32, and so on to become a fetus with many billions of cells.

One clue to the inheritance of traits came from the study of sperm from the male and ova from the female. Studies with microscopes showed that a sperm and an ovum each has one set of the rod-shaped bodies that came to be called chromosomes.

A page from Mendel's notebook describes crosses between different kinds of beans.

Under the microscope, each cell resulting from the union of a sperm and an ovum was seen to have a small central body, the nucleus. And each nucleus of these cells had two sets of chromosomes. The chromosomes reproduced themselves in each cell division so that each new cell in turn had two sets of chromosomes. The name for these molecules is based on their affinity for colored dyes—*chromos* means "color" in Greek—which had been shown in experiments done in the 1870s by a German biologist, Walther Flemming. He found that just before a cell divides to form two cells, in a process that is called mitosis, each chromosome (which he dyed red, to make it visible under the microscope) grows fatter until it divides into two chromosomes. One of each of the reproduced chromosomes goes into each of the two new cells, giving them a full set of chromosomes.

It was Walter S. Sutton, a scientist at Columbia University in New York, who proposed that the behavior of the chromosomes made them the logical choice to be the carriers of Mendel's elements, or genes. Sutton was studying the formation of grasshopper sex cells. He noticed that the chromosomes in these cells behaved just the way Mendel's "elements" were supposed to behave. Working with the fruit fly *(Drosophila melanogaster),* Sutton found that one trait, eye color, was linked to sex. The gene for eye color thus had to be carried on the sex chromosome, Sutton argued. The logical consequence of that finding, he added, was that chromosomes carried the genes for all traits. Sutton's work, which was soon generally accepted, won him many honors.

The number of chromosomes in a cell differs from species to species. There are 46 in humans (two pairs of 23) but just eight (two pairs of four) in the fruit fly. Given the large number of traits in fruit flies as well as humans, it was obvious that each chromosome contained a large number of genes, which explained why two or more traits could be inherited together: Their genes are on the same chromosome. What remained to be determined was the chemical nature of the gene and the chromosome, and the structure that allowed the transmission of specific traits from one generation to another.

Four major substances are found in living beings—proteins, polysaccharides (sugars and starches), lipids (fats), and nucleic acids. The nucleic acids were the last to be identified. The work that led to nucleic acids being added to the list began in 1868, when Johann Miescher, a 24-year-old Swiss chemist, went to Germany to study in the laboratory of Ernst Hoppe-Seyler, a prominent chemist.

Miescher concentrated on the composition of the cell nucleus, which can clearly be seen under the microscope in most cells. He obtained his nuclei from white blood cells, which have large nuclei, and the blood cells out of pus in surgical bandages from a hospital in the city of Tubingen. By 1869 he had isolated a substance from the nuclei of these blood cells that was rich in phosphorus, was apparently made up of very large molecules, and was acidic. (An acid is a substance that releases hydrogen ions, which carry positive electrical charges, when it is placed in water.) Miescher called this substance nuclein.

Miescher continued his work on nuclein when he returned to Switzerland the next year. Now he was able to obtain his cell nuclei from a less repellent source, the sperm of salmon that lived in the Rhine. He soon found that nuclein was actually a combination of proteins and nucleic acids—the term *nucleic acid* was not coined until 1889.

By the end of the century, the composition of the nucleic acids studied by Miescher had been determined. Nucleic acid molecules have three constituents. One is a phosphate, a phosphorus atom with four oxygen atoms attached. A second is a sugar called ribose, built of five carbon atoms in a ring (ordinary table sugar has a six-carbon ring). The third is called a base.

Bases are made up of nitrogen and carbon atoms and come in several varieties. Five in all have been identified: adenine, guanine, cytosine, thymine, and uracil. They are flat in shape. In DNA, the bases lie at right angles to the rest of the nucleic acid molecule, a backbone made up of a long sequence of phosphates. Guanine and adenine, called the purines, have double rings, made of carbon and nitrogen atoms, with four hydrogen atoms attached to the four carbon atoms in each ring. The two bases are distinguished by the different side groups of atoms that branch off from the carbon atoms in the ring. Thymine, cytosine, and uracil, called the pyrimidines, have single rings made of carbon and nitrogen atoms. Again, each base is distinguished by having a different side group branching off from the carbon atoms of the ring.

In a few years, it was found that there are two kinds of nucleic acid. In one of them the ribose has one less oxygen atom than in the other; it is called dexoxyribose nucleic acid, DNA. The other is ribonucleic acid, RNA. The bases in RNA are adenine, guanine, cytosine, and uracil. In DNA, thymine replaces uracil.

It was just before Miescher did his work that Gregor Mendel published the results of his research. It took some time for the two research efforts to be put together in a coherent picture.

MENDELIAN GENETICS

G regor Mendel worked with a relatively simple organism, the garden pea, and in his most important experiments studied just a few traits—two colors (yellow and green), two plant lengths (long and short), and two types of seeds (round or wrinkled).

Mendel first obtained seeds that yielded only one variety of each trait that he studied. For example, a round seed from a tall, yellow plant would grow into a tall, yellow plant with round seeds.

His next step was to cross-pollinate different kinds of these plants, crossing a plant with a round seed and a plant with a wrinkled seed, a short plant with a tall plant, a green plant with a yellow plant.

In the first generation of plants from these cross-pollinations (the F1 generation, as it is now called), the plants bred true, with only one version of each trait emerging. But, notably, some traits that were found in the original plants were not seen in crossbred plants of the F1 generation. The plants would be either all yellow or all green, all short or all tall, and with all wrinkled or all round seeds. There were no plants that mixed the different characteristics of the parent plants with, say, some wrinkled and some round seeds in the same plant.

When these F1 plants reproduced, the second, or F2, generation was different again. Some of the traits that had disappeared in the first generation reemerged. An

text continues on page 34

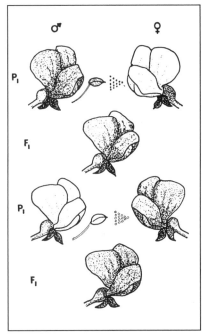

Reciprocal crosses between purple-flower and white-flower varieties in the garden pea. In the top cross the purple-flower plant provides pollen; in the bottom cross the white-flower plant provides pollen.

text continued from page 33

F1 plant with wrinkled seeds could have offspring with round seeds, for example. But, again, there was no mixing: Each plant still was all yellow or all green, or had either all wrinkled or all round seeds, for example.

Mendel then applied mathematics in a simple way, counting the numbers of the different traits in the plants of the F2 generation. He recorded that there were 5,474 plants with round seeds but only 1,850 with wrinkled seeds, and 6,022 yellow plants and 2,001 green plants—in each case, a ratio of about 3 to 1.

Using these ratios, Mendel formulated certain rules, or laws, that he believed guided heredity. To begin with, he proposed that each adult plant contained two units, which he called elements (and we call genes), that controlled each trait. He also hypothesized that an element could exist in one of two versions, strong or weak. The strong element was dominant over the weak element.

Mendel's rules said that a plant that inherited two strong elements would have the strong trait. And a plant that inherited one strong element and one weak one for a trait would also have the strong trait. Only if a plant inherited two weak elements would it have the weak trait. This formulation explained the 3 to 1 ratio that Mendel had observed. Today, we call Mendel's strong element a dominant gene and a weak element a recessive gene.

One of the most important observations Mendel made, which is embodied in his laws, was that the elements for the traits are inherited independently. Inheriting one trait is not dependent on inheriting another. In other words, each element is passed from generation to generation separately from the elements for other traits. Having round seeds, for example, did not influence the color of a plant, because the two traits were governed by different genes.

One basic finding of Mendel's studies was that genes alone, not the environment, governed inheritance. This rule was challenged by a then-popular theory proposed by a French scientist, Jean-Baptiste Lamarck. He argued that when the environment of an organism like an animal changed, the organism changed to adapt to the new environment, and if the environment changed back, so did the organism. Traits caused by the environment could be passed to the next generation, Lamarck said.

Lamarckism, as it was called, was immensely popular, because it provided a simple explanation for the differences between species that everyone could understand. But it was disproved by an equally simple experiment done by a German zoologist, August Weismann. When he cut off the tails of hundreds of mice and allowed the mice to reproduce,

Jean-Baptiste Lamarck coined the word biology and devised an early theory of evolution that argued that organisms change in order to adapt to new environments.

all of their offspring had tails. Weismann concluded that this experiment showed that whatever governed reproduction was totally separate from the rest of the body and followed different rules from those proposed by Lamarck. Mendel had already discovered these rules, however, although no one knew it yet.

Mendel sent copies of the paper he had written to a number of scientists, but they were ignored. He read his findings to the local scientific society, without arousing much interest. The paper was published in the society's rather obscure scientific journal, but no one in the larger world of science paid attention. Then Mendel soon became the head of his monastery, which required him to give up most of his scientific studies. When he died in 1884, his discoveries were still generally unrecognized.

The Emergence of Nucleic Acids

When Watson and Crick began to work on DNA, the question of its structure was one of the leading issues in biology. It had not always been that way. The function of nucleic acids such as DNA remained unclear for some time after they were first described. It was generally assumed at the time that genes were made up of proteins, because proteins have structures that seemed to make them potentially capable of carrying the vast amounts of information needed for the reproduction of living things.

The basic unit of a protein is a molecular chain made up of subunits called amino acids. More than 20 amino acids can be found in various cells, and a protein can consist of amino acids in any number and in any sequence. Some proteins have more than one chain of amino acid. This complexity is in sharp contrast to the nucleic acids, each of which has just four subunits. This limited variety of subunits made nucleic acids seem like improbable candidates for the genetic substance, because they did not seem to have the information-carrying capacity of proteins. Indeed, a prevailing belief was that each unit of nucleic acid consisted of an assemblage of all four bases and that this tetranu-

Oswald T. Avery, a bacteriologist at the Rockefeller Institute in New York, identified DNA as the material of genes during his studies of bacteria.

cleotide, as it was called, repeated itself monotonously, leaving it no opportunity to carry biological information.

This view changed dramatically in the 1940s because of research done first by a researcher in England named Frederick Griffith and later at the Rockefeller Institute in New York by Oswald T. Avery and his colleagues. Avery's effort was built on work done years before by Griffith, a doctor doing research at England's Ministry of Health on pneumococcus bacteria. These bacteria come in two forms, one called smooth because under the microscope it can be seen to be surrounded by a glossy capsule, the other called rough, because it has no such capsule. Smooth (S) pneumococci are killers. When they infect a laboratory animal, that animal dies quickly. Rough (R) pneumococci are relatively harmless. When they infect an animal, it generally survives.

What Griffith did was to inject into the same mice both a small amount of living (and harmless) R bacteria and a large quantity of S bacteria that had been killed by heat. Many of these mice died; in them Griffith found living, infectious S bacteria. Something had transformed the harmless R bacteria into deadly live S bacteria. People doubted Griffith's work at first, but it was soon confirmed by experiments in other laboratories, including Avery's. The question Avery set out to answer was the identity of the transforming factor, the material that had changed the genetic character of the R bacteria, in effect bringing dead cells back to life.

At the beginning, Avery believed that the transforming factor was a protein of some sort. To test this belief, he and his colleagues began a careful, methodical series of studies. After growing large amount of bacteria in vats, Griffith killed them, and in a decisive series of tests exposed the transforming factor to enzymes, which are proteins that can break up proteins and other natural molecules. When Griffith used enzymes known to digest proteins, however, the transforming factor remained active. But when he used an enzyme known to digest DNA (called DNAase; -*ase* is the standard suffix for an enzyme, a protein that regulates a chemical reaction in the body), the activity of the transforming factor was destroyed.

These and other tests established that the transforming factor—the gene of the streptococcus—was made of DNA. In a letter to his brother, Roy, Avery wrote that this "means that nucleic acids are not merely structurally important but functionally active substances in determining the biochemical activities and specific characteristics of cells . . . it is possible to induce predictable and hereditary changes in cells. . . . Sounds like a virus—may be a gene."

Avery made this observation in a private letter. In public, however, he was hesitant to publish his findings. When he finally did publish them in a scientific paper, its language was very cautious. This caution probably cost him a Nobel Prize; he died shortly after the paper was published and before the confirming experiments he seemed to insist on could be done.

The question remained, though, of how DNA carried genetic information. DNA seemed to be a molecule without the diversity needed to carry the immense amount of information required to govern a living being. The tetranuclear hypothesis, which said that DNA is a monotonous molecule in which four bases are repeated indefinitely, was hardly a prescription for an information-carrying molecule.

The answer came from a scientist named Erwin Chargaff, whose work was an inspiration to Watson and Crick, according to a story Watson tells in his book, *The Double Helix*. Watson relates that one evening in a pub, when Francis Crick was chatting with John Griffith, a theoretical chemist, they began debating how genes copied themselves. They had just attended an astronomy lecture on "The Perfect Cosmological Principle" and were debating whether there could be a "perfect biological principle."

Griffith's idea was a sort of lock-and-key theory, in which a new gene was formed by fitting itself to the surface of the original gene. Crick countered with a proposal that there were specific attractive forces between the flat surfaces of the DNA bases, and that molecular attractions between the atoms on the edges of specific bases enabled a matching up of the bases of the new gene to those of the original gene. This explanation, which was one of biological action in terms of physics, turned out to be right. Griffith was soon able to report to Crick that he had done the calculations and that adenine attracted thymine and guanine attracted cytosine, according to the rule devised by Erwin Chargaff. He had determined that in DNA there was always the same amount of thymine and adenine (suggesting that they were somehow paired) and the same occurred with guanine and cytosine, although the abundance of the guanine–cytosine abundance could be different from the adenine–thymine abundance.

However good a story this is, Crick later wrote, "I am confident that I was not aware of Chargaff's rule at that time, even if Jim [Watson] had, as he claimed, mentioned them to me earlier. If he had told me I had simply forgotten them."

Chargaff, at the College of Physicians and Surgeons of Columbia University in New York, had been inspired by Avery's paper. Chargaff later wrote that "Avery gave us the first text of a new language, or rather he showed where to look for it. I resolved to search for this text."

The method Chargaff used was a new technique called paper chromatography. The first step in it is to expose a number of molecules of DNA to something that will chop each molecule into separate components, isolating the bases. Then the solution containing the chopped-up DNA is absorbed by a sheet of filter paper. Each base comes to rest at a different location on the filter paper. The spots containing each base are then cut off and the bases are washed off the paper so that their concentrations can be measured.

This was not an easy enterprise for Chargaff, who first had to develop many of the necessary techniques. Not until 1950 was he able to publish a paper describing his results. That paper dwelt on his finding that the four DNA bases occur in widely differing proportions in different species. But it also noted that no differences had been found in DNA from the nuclei of ordinary cells and of sperm cells. Chargaff's paper killed the tetranuclear hypothesis, but it left alive the question of how DNA could carry and transmit genetic information.

The ultimate answer, as it turned out, lay in one sentence of Chargaff's paper: "It is, however, noteworthy— whether this is more than accidental, cannot yet be said— that in all deoxypentose nucleic acids [DNAs] examined thus far the . . . ratios of . . . adenine to thymine and of guanine to cytosine were not far from 1."

So for each A (adenine) there was a T (thymine), for each G (guanine) a C (cytosine). Chargaff did not carry this observation any further, but it opened doors for other researchers. One of them was Francis Crick, according to Jim Watson's version of the story.

Whatever the actual story, Chargaff's contribution was essential to the eventual solution of the DNA puzzle. But his was just one contribution among the many that were made by a scientific cast of characters that covered nearly half the globe.

Another of them was Sir Lawrence Bragg, the head of the Cavendish Laboratory at Cambridge University, under whom Watson and Crick did their crucial work on DNA.

Nearly four decades earlier, Bragg had originated X-ray diffraction, the technique of determining the structure of

This woman monitors a punch-card instrument for X-ray diffraction, which is used to determine molecular structure.

solid molecules by exposing them to X rays and analyzing the resulting shadows that were cast as the X rays bounced off crystals of the molecules. (A crystal is a regular, organized collection of molecules.)

X-ray diffraction works through analysis of the patterns created when X rays are directed through a crystal of the molecule that is being studied. Suppose that two or more beams of X rays are aimed at a crystal. The two beams are reflected in slightly different ways as they pass through the crystal, and the resulting diffraction pattern, as it is called, is captured on photographic paper. By studying one or more of these diffraction patterns, it is possible to determine the position of the atoms and the distances between them in the crystal. The more complicated the molecule, of course, the more difficult it is to determine its structure.

His development of X-ray crystallography made Bragg the youngest person ever to win a Nobel Prize. He won it when he was just 25 years old. Then, when he became head of the Cavendish Laboratory, Bragg engineered a remarkable change there, one that allowed Watson and Crick to join the laboratory.

Traditionally, the Cavendish Laboratory had specialized in experimental physics. Bragg expanded its role in two directions that were apparently unrelated but had a common theme. One was radioastronomy. With Bragg's encouragement, a young physicist named Martin Ryle built the world's first radio telescope, which received radiowave emissions from the heavens. This work led to the dis-

This X-ray diffraction pattern of a form of DNA was obtained by Maurice Wilkins, who was the first to produce these images.

covery of strange and then-unknown objects in the universe—pulsars, neutron stars, quasars, and the like—which revolutionized astronomy.

Bragg also led the laboratory toward the investigation of crystals of biological molecules by X-ray diffraction. Seemingly worlds apart from radio astronomy, this work resembled it in that it required the analysis of strange patterns—in one case from objects in the universe, in the other of biological molecules in the laboratory. It was this change, engineered by Bragg, that enabled Crick and Watson to study DNA at the Cavendish.

A key figure in the investigation of biological molecules by X-ray diffraction was Max Perutz. It was Perutz who developed a method for applying Bragg's X-ray crystallographic techniques, which originally were used only on molecules important to physics, to the study of biological molecules. Years later, Perutz recalled that "when I showed him (Bragg) my X-ray pictures of hemoglobin his face lit up," and that when Bragg verified that the method could be used to determine the structure of proteins "tears streamed down his face."

But not all the actors in the story of DNA were at the Cavendish Laboratory. At King's College in London there was Maurice Wilkins, another physicist who had switched to biology after the war and had become a leading researcher in DNA. Wilkins played a crucial role in the discovery of DNA structure—so crucial that he eventually shared the Nobel Prize awarded to Watson and Crick. He was an expert in crystallography and had some of the world's best equipment for working with it. One of his crucial discoveries was that the molecules of life, such as DNA, could have a crystal structure. As he said in formal scientific language at a meeting in Italy in 1951, "When living matter is to be found in the crystalline state, the possibility is increased of molecular interpretation of biological structure and processes. In particular, the study of crystalline nucleoproteins in living cells may help one to approach more closely the problem of gene structure."

Jim Watson was one of the people in the audience at that meeting. Wilkins's talk excited him, because Watson had been worried that genes might have irregular structures that would make them immensely difficult to study. Wilkins's discovery eliminated that depressing possibility. And Watson would be in Cambridge, not far from Wilkins's laboratory in London.

But Wilkins was not working alone. Rosalind Franklin, a talented crystallographer, was also working at King's College on the use of X-ray crystallography to determine the structure of DNA. Franklin and Wilkins were far from being friends; their conflicts are among the most publicized disputes in the history of modern science.

Rosalind Franklin had studied chemistry at Cambridge and had been working on the crystallography of coal, first in England and later in France. By common agreement of the people who knew her, she was a tough-minded lady, used to speaking her mind bluntly. The dominant impression she gave was of scientific professionalism and firmness of mind. She was slim and short, with thick, glossy black hair and bright eyes, and dressed sensibly and neatly. She came to King's College in 1951, when she was about 30 years old, because she was interested in applying crystallography to the study of the structure of biological molecules, including DNA.

Because she was a woman, Franklin encountered various annoyances when she moved from France to King's College. For example, she and other women on the faculty were not allowed to use the common room, where male faculty members could relax. This discrimination was one of the reasons why she moved in 1953 to Birkbeck College, where she continued to work on DNA.

Wilkins's understanding was that Rosalind Franklin had been hired to help him learn more about the X-ray diffraction techniques that were needed to work out the DNA structure problem. His idea was that they would work in collaboration. But in 1951, about the time that Watson arrived at Cambridge, Franklin said she would not collaborate with Wilkins. She insisted that the task of determining the structure of DNA had been assigned to her alone. Her insistence on this point started a long-running quarrel between Wilkins and Franklin.

Indeed, the conflict between Wilkins and Franklin soon assumed almost legendary proportions. "Almost from the moment she arrived in Maurice's lab, they began to upset each other," Watson noted. "Maurice, a beginner in X-ray diffraction work, wanted some professional help and hoped that Rosy, a trained crystallographer, could speed up the research. Rosy, however, did not see the situation this way. She claimed that she had been given DNA for her own problem and would not think of herself as Maurice's assistant."

The conflict was to persist virtually until Franklin's untimely death of cancer in 1958, at the age of 37. By then, she had come very close to discovering the structure of DNA. The X-ray diffraction patterns she obtained were perhaps the most important clues to the determination of that structure.

Franklin also worked with Watson and Crick—and had her differences with Watson. Over the years, the controversy over the role she played in the discovery of the double helix has never ended. The generally accepted view is that she never made the last, decisive step that would have allowed her to describe the structure of DNA. But there are those who believe that Franklin did enough significant work to deserve a major place in scientific history, and that she has unjustly been deprived of the honors awarded to other scientists working on the DNA problem.

In his book, Watson paints a grotesque picture of Rosalind Franklin, saying that "there was never lipstick to contrast with her black hair, while at the age of 31 her dresses showed all the imagination of English blue-stocking adolescents." This description was not in fact a true picture of her. Franklin did have a hard outer shell when working, but friends testify that she could be delightful when she relaxed. As a scientist, she had the kind of single-minded intensity that often is praised in male scientists, especially those working in the field of genetics.

Franklin and Watson and Crick became part of a world-wide (and quite informal) web of scientists at the forefront of genetic research. In the United States there was also Salvatore Luria, who had been the great influence on Watson at the University of Indiana. Luria was a member of a circle of researchers, scattered throughout the United States and Europe, who called themselves the "phage group" because they were doing work on a group of viruses that infect bacteria—bacteriophage, or phage for short—viruses.

The great advantage of working with a phage virus is the relative simplicity of its genetic system. A bacteriophage is made of protein and nucleic acid. When a phage virus meets a single bacterial cell, it attaches itself to the cell and injects its genetic material into it. The genetic material then commandeers the reproductive system of the bacterial cell and goes to work making phage viruses. In as little as 20 minutes, the original bacterial cell is dead and up to 200 new phage viruses will have emerged to infect other bacteria and repeat the process. The "phage group" consisted of scientists at a number of laboratories who were working with these viruses. Jim Watson had become a member of the group at the University of Indiana and still maintained close ties with many of its members.

About the time that Watson began to work with Crick, he got a letter from a member of the phage group, Alfred Hershey, that explained many puzzling things about bacteriophage viruses. The critical study that Hershey did with a

colleague, Martha Chase, soon became famous as the "Waring Blendor experiment."

The object of the study was to determine the roles of the two kinds of molecule, protein and DNA, that make up a phage virus. Hershey and Chase started by growing phage viruses in two culture mediums—one containing radioactive phosphorus, the other radioactive sulfur. Because phosphorus is an essential element in DNA but sulfur is never found there, only the radioactive phosphorus would be in the phage DNA. Similarly, only the radioactive sulfur would be found in the protein.

Then they infected bacterial cells with the two kinds of specially prepared phage viruses. One kind contained only radioactive sulfur, the marker for protein. The other held only radioactive phosphorus, the marker for DNA. The next step was to break up the infected bacterial cells to see

The phage group at the California Institute of Technology in 1949. From left: Jean Weigle, Ole Maaløe, Elie Wollman, Gunther Stent, Max Delbrück, and Giorgio Soli.

if they contained protein or DNA. Finding protein would mean that it carried the genetic information of the phage virus. Finding DNA would identify it as the carrier of genetic information.

The experiment ran into trouble when Hershey and Chase could not find a good way to separate the various molecular components. Eventually, they put the cells into a Waring Blendor, which worked just fine for separating the components. Hershey and Chase found that the sulfur-bearing protein remained in the liquid outside the cell, while the phosphorus-bearing DNA was left inside the cell. This finding showed that DNA, not protein, was the carrier of phage genetic information. Watson later summed up the finding by saying that DNA was "the hat inside the hatbox," with protein serving just as the virus's container for the DNA.

Such work raised the immediate question of how DNA carried genetic information. What in the structure of DNA made it possible for it to transmit all the traits of a living thing from generation to generation? And this question raised a further one: What made it possible for the changes called mutations to occur in the genetic makeup of an organism, as, for example, when a virus or a bacterium developed resistance to a drug? Watson and Crick were not the only scientists to address those questions.

The Waring Blendor that Alfred Hershey and Martha Chase used in their pivotal experiment was named after Fred Waring, a society bandleader of the 1930s and 1940s. Waring did not directly invent the machine, but he made it happen—and made it famous.

The story began in 1936, when Waring and his band, the Pennsylvanians, had just finished a radio broadcast in Manhattan's Vanderbilt Theater. Waring was approached by a promoter-inventor named Fred Osius, who had an idea for a new and revolutionary (literally) kitchen mixer. Osius did not even have a working model, but the idea captured Waring's attention enough that he agreed to put up money for its development.

After six months and $25,000, Osius still did not have a working model, so Waring stepped in and turned the project over to one of his associates. The "Miracle Mixer," the first working kitchen blender, was introduced at the National Restaurant Show in Chicago in September 1937. The machine became a hit and inspired the development of other blenders over the next few years. Waring was careful to spell his blender's trade name with an "o" for the Waring Blendor, to distinguish it from all the others. After World War II, Waring Products established its manufacturing facility in Connecticut, where the Blendor is still being made.

Hershey and Chase were not the only medical scientists to use the Blendor. Jonas Salk used one to help prepare materials that he used to develop the polio vaccine. The Blendor today has competition from many other blenders, but it still holds its place in medical and scientific history.

Dressed in formal attire, winners of the 1962 Nobel Prizes display their diplomas after ceremonies in Stockholm's Concert Hall. Watson (second from right), Crick (third from left), and Wilkins (far left) shared the Nobel Prize for Medicine for establishing the structure of DNA, the molecule responsible for transmitting hereditary information.

The Emergence of the Double Helix

The collaboration between James Watson and Francis Crick is an example of a major change that was then occurring in the study of living things. Watson had followed the traditional pathway toward that study, majoring in biology in college and afterward in his graduate studies. But Crick came from an entirely different scientific background. His training was in physics, yet he was applying that knowledge to research on the nature of life. Other physicists and chemists were following the same route, studying the molecules of life as they would any other molecules. It was the birth of the new discipline that has come to be called molecular biology.

No single person represented the importance of that change more than a chemist who lived far from Cambridge: Linus Carl Pauling, who was based at the California Institute of Technology. Pauling began as a straightforward chemist but became one of the major players in molecular biology. As they began their work on DNA, Watson and Crick were aware that their chief competitor in the race to discover its molecular structure was Pauling.

Linus Pauling had spent a long lifetime studying the structure of molecules, embodying his knowledge in such major books as *The Nature of the Chemical Bond* (1939). He was awarded the Nobel Prize for chemistry in 1954 for "his work on the nature of the chemical bond and its application to the elucidation of the structure of complex substances."

The chemical bond that makes atoms and molecules stick together is a result of the electrical charges that the atoms carry. Some are positive, some negative. Atoms come together to form molecules when positively charged atoms in one molecule attract negatively charged atoms in another molecule, so that the resulting atoms combine in such a way that these electrical charges must be neutralized both over the entire molecule and also in local areas.

There can be two major kinds of chemical bond in biological molecules: double, or strong, bonds; and single, or weak, bonds. (There are also triple bonds, but they are rare.) In a double bond, two atoms of the molecule share two electrons. In a single bond, they share one electron. Double bonds are shorter than single bonds and are also less flexible; their atoms are less able to swing to different positions.

The situation becomes more complex as the size of a biological molecule and the number of its bonds increase. In a biological molecule, there can be alternating double and single bonds. But those bonds are not constant. There is a principle called resonance, which says that bonds can swing back and forth between atoms in such a molecule. A single bond and a double bond change position, then switch back to their original positions. All this takes place in the smallest fraction of a second and over incredibly tiny distances that are measured in angstrom units. To give you some idea how small the world of atomic bonds is, one angstrom unit is about four billionths of an inch.

There are weaker bonds as well, in which the electrical charges of atoms influence one another. One is called a hydrogen bond, in which a portion of the negative charge of a hydrogen atom forms a weak, easily broken link with the positive charge of a neighboring atom. Another is the van der Waals force, named after a Dutch physicist, in which oppositely charged atoms affect each other's electrical charges slightly.

Although Linus Pauling helped clarify the nature and roles of these bonds, his towering achievement was the description of a specific kind of protein structure, the alpha helix, in which an understanding of the hydrogen bond was an essential key. The way in which he discovered it was about as influential as the discovery itself when the hunt for the structure of DNA began.

The first question about proteins was whether the amino acids that are their structural units are simply piled together or are assembled in some organized way. By the mid–1930s, studies were indicating that there was an organized protein structure, but its nature was unclear. Pauling and several other chemists got the answer to that question at about the same time: Proteins are chains of amino acids, with the amino acids held together by strong links called peptide bonds. ("Peptide" comes from the word *pepsin,* the name of an enzyme that can sever the bonds and break up protein chains.) Thus, a protein can also be called a polypeptide chain.

Data from X-ray crystallography studies indicated that a protein chain often had a coiled structure. Working with an associate, Robert Corey, Pauling set out to determine the exact nature of that coil. A crucial part of the effort was the method they used. Instead of applying abstract techniques, Pauling and Corey constructed extremely precise metal models of the peptide units that make up a protein chain. They used little metal figures cut exactly in the shapes of the different elements that made up proteins, then put them together in much the same way someone would a jigsaw puzzle. The metal models had to be crafted with great care, because an error of even a small fraction of an inch would have invalidated the results. As he later explained, Pauling turned to physical models because "the analytical treatment is so complex as to resist successful execution, and only the model method can be used." Pauling's use of these models had a great influence on Watson and Crick when they began working out the structure of DNA a few years later.

Pauling knew that the peptides in the protein chain were connected by double bonds between a carbon atom of one peptide and a nitrogen atom of the next peptide in line.

Linus Pauling (left) and his assistant, Robert Corey, with a model of a molecule. Pauling discovered the alpha helix, the polypeptide configuration of proteins.

The models of the peptides that he and Corey made were accordingly built to fit that understanding.

The breakthrough came when Pauling left California to be a visiting professor at Oxford in 1948. As he later told the story, he caught a cold in the chilly British spring weather and went to bed. Bored, he began to draw pictures of how a polypeptide chain would look if it were perfectly flat, with all its atoms on a single plane. As he looked at the diagram, he realized that the structure he wanted for a chain of peptide units was not flat but was instead probably a spiraling coil—a helix. When he folded the paper to make such a helix, he saw that the coiled molecular structure of the chain could be held together by hydrogen bonds between a hydrogen atom in one peptide and an oxygen atom in a peptide two or three units away in the chain.

Over the next few years, Pauling and Corey worked to refine their discovery and make it scientifically watertight. They published their work in a short paper in the *Journal of the American Chemical Society* in October 1950, showing a chain of peptides that coiled to the right, with each full turn of the spiral containing exactly 3.6 peptide units. By then, Pauling had given the polypeptide configuration a name: the alpha helix.

In April 1951, Pauling and Corey published seven more scientific papers that expanded on their discovery. These papers described the structure of such proteins as hair, feathers, silk, muscle, tendons, and hemoglobin. They also analyzed two other configurations for proteins. One of them, which they called "pleated sheet," was described as a flat, layered structure that has since been found to be part of many proteins.

Pauling and Corey also proposed a structure for collagen, a flexible, tough protein found in bones, tendons, and tusks, as well as the cornea of the eye. They suggested that collagen was a three-stranded helix—a proposal that turned out to be completely wrong.

Pauling and Corey's protein papers had an enormous impact on biologists, including Crick and Watson. Crick later said that Pauling's work taught him several lessons, including the importance of model building in trying to determine molecular structure, and the need to be bold when making theories in molecular biology. For Jim Watson, these Pauling papers had a strong emotional impact.

In his book, *The Double Helix,* Watson wrote that in the pursuit of the structure of DNA it was always Pauling whom he pictured himself competing with. "There was no one like Linus in all the world," Watson wrote. "The combination of his prodigious mind and infectious grin was unbeatable." Watson also wrote a malicious description of a meeting in California at which Pauling supposedly displayed the structure of DNA, calling it "dazzling and full of rhetorical tricks." But the description was entirely imaginary, since Watson was not at the meeting; it was designed to run down Pauling's reputation.

One important event that Maurice Wilkins told Watson about was a new finding that Franklin had just made. Wilkins spoke as the two men walked down the hallway in Cambridge.

Rosalind Franklin did not discover the structure of DNA. Yet one of her findings—the one that Wilkins told Watson about that day in Cambridge—proved to be of vital importance. She had discovered that fibers of DNA could give two distinct types of X-ray diffraction patterns. Wilkins had found that moderately wet fibers of DNA produced diffraction patterns suggesting that they had a crystalline structure. Franklin found that when a lot more water was added to the DNA fibers they produced a different kind of X-ray diffraction pattern. She called the less-wet DNA Type A and the wetter form Type B. The difference between these two types of DNA turned out to be of vital importance in Watson and Crick's determination of DNA structure.

Several questions remained to be answered in determining the structure of DNA. One concerned the position of its phosphate backbone. Putting it on the inside of the molecule seemed to make sense. If the bases carried genetic information, having them stick out from the backbone would make it easier for them to transfer their information inside the cell. Then there was the question of how the bases carried the genetic information that governed the function of the cell. Finally, it still needed to be determined how the molecules of the cell used the information contained in the genes to make the proteins that are essential to cell function.

None of this was known when Watson and Crick began their collaboration in 1952. The answers, everyone was convinced, lay in the interpretation of the X-ray diffraction patterns of DNA. Here, Watson and Crick (and Wilkins and Franklin) had an advantage. The English laboratories, in Cambridge and London, had X-ray diffraction equipment that was better than what was available to Pauling and other American researchers. The clearer X-ray diffraction patterns that were produced in England made it easier to determine the nature of the DNA molecule.

Pauling was working hard on DNA, however. Toward the end of 1952, Watson and Crick were told that Pauling had worked out the structure of DNA. A scientific paper describing that structure was published in February 1953. It proved to be spectacularly wrong.

The Pauling paper described DNA as "a three-chain structure, each chain being a helix." The distance between nucleotides in each helix was calculated at 3.4 angstroms, and each helix was supposed to make a complete turn every 27.2 angstroms.

Most important, Pauling placed the phosphate backbones of the DNA structure in the interior of the molecule. One reason he gave for doing so was that putting the bases inside the structure would make the molecule too irregular. Another was that "it is important for the stability of the molecule that atoms be well packed together."

Almost immediately, everyone—including Pauling—began to see that there were major problems with this proposed structure. One flaw in the model was that the atoms were packed too tightly together to meet the basic chemical requirements. Another was that it pictured the hydrogen atoms as being tightly bound to the phosphate groups. Watson knew that the hydrogen atoms could not be too solidly packed, because an acid is defined as a molecule that can release hydrogen atoms. "Pauling's nucleic acid in a sense was not an acid at all," Watson realized. And finally, the Pauling model did not explain how the DNA structure he was proposing carried and transferred its genetic information. Another story told in Watson's book, *The Double Helix,* concerns the reaction that Rosalind Franklin had when she was shown the Pauling paper. As Watson told the story, he asked if she wanted to see the newly arrived manuscript. Franklin became annoyed, the story went on, and began lecturing Watson on helical theory, saying that "not a shred of evidence permitted Linus, or anyone else, to postulate a helical structure for DNA."

"Suddenly Rosy came from behind the lab bench that separated us and began moving toward me," Watson wrote. "Fearing that in her hot anger she might strike me, I grabbed up the Pauling manuscript and hastily retreated to the open door."

This is a comical picture, which is even funnier if one remembers that Watson was well over six feet tall and Franklin was short, slim, and hardly a physical threat. Many of Franklin's defenders say that Watson deliberately exaggerated the scene to make Franklin look ridiculous.

The scene ended when Wilkins came into the room. The two men left together and, as they walked down the corridor, Watson told Wilkins that Franklin had come close to assaulting him. "Slowly he assured me that this might very well have happened," Watson wrote. "Some months

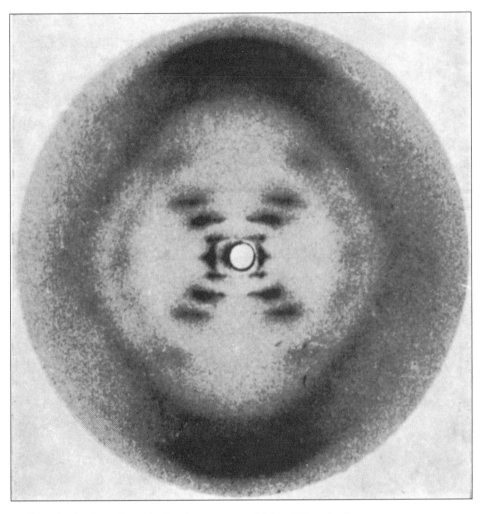

earlier she had made a similar lunge toward him. They had almost come to blows following an argument in his room."

So went the story in *The Double Helix*, a tale that brought Watson heavy criticism. In later editions of the book, Watson added an apology to Franklin, who by then was no longer alive.

Watson went to London when the Pauling paper was published to show it to Wilkins and Franklin. The scene he describes is one of the dramatic moments of his book—not because of the Pauling paper but because of what Watson learned on that visit. At the meeting, Wilkins told Watson

This X-ray diffraction pattern of the B form of DNA at high humidity was obtained by Rosalind Franklin.

of a new X-ray diffraction picture that Franklin had made of the B form of DNA. Watson asked to see it.

"The instant I saw the picture my mouth fell open and my pulse began to race," Watson wrote. "The pattern was unbelievably simpler than those obtained previously. Moreover, the black cross of reflections which dominated the picture could arise only from a helical structure."

On a later trip to London with Watson to have dinner with Wilkins, Crick emphasized that they were in a close race with Pauling. "If he put one of his assistants to taking DNA photographs, the B structure would also be discovered in Pasadena," Watson wrote. "Then, in a week at most, Linus would have the structure."

On the train ride back to Cambridge, Watson began drawing sketches of possible DNA structures, either two-chain or three-chain models. It was late, so he could not use the main entrance to the college to get to his room. "By the time I had cycled back to college and climbed over the back gate, I had decided to build two-chain models," he wrote. "Francis would have to agree. Even though he was a physicist, he knew that important biological objects come in pairs." Crick did not agree at first, but Watson kept on working on two- and three-chain DNA structures, concentrating on two-chain models.

While all this was going on, Watson and Crick were waiting for the machine shop at the Cavendish Laboratory to make the metal forms of the phosphates and bases they needed to construct a DNA model. As Watson later described that time, he was working with cardboard cutouts on DNA models with the phosphate backbones inside, because putting the backbones on the outside would raise "the frightful problem" of how to fit the bases inside the molecule. One possibility that he suggested to Crick was that the purine bases could pair with each other, and the pyrimidine bases could pair in the same way—adenine with adenine, guanine with guanine—and so on. But Crick rejected that model, for several reasons. One was that both chains of bases would have to run in the same direction, which did not fit in with the X-ray diffraction evidence. Another was that it did not explain the one-to-one Chargaff ratios of the bases. These ratios state that the amount of adenine is always the same as the amount of thymine, and the amount of guanine is always the same as the amount of cytosine.

As Watson tried to build two-chain models, he ran into several major problems. One was that the four bases had quite different shapes: two were big, two small. Another was that the sequence of bases in a DNA chain was irregular. It seemed that twisting two DNA chains around each other would give a messy result. In some places the bigger bases would touch each other, so a two-chain DNA molecule would bulge out in that area. In other places the smaller bases would face each other, so the molecular structure would buckle in.

There was also the question of how the intertwined chains would be held together by hydrogen bonds between the bases. "Conceivably, the crux of the matter was a rule governing hydrogen bonding between bases," Watson wrote.

He apparently solved that problem a few days later, when he noted that each adenine could form the needed hydrogen bonds with another adenine that was opposite to it in the DNA structure; the same would be true of hydrogen bonds between pairs of the other bases. Watson's first picture of a DNA molecule consisting of two chains, each with the same sequence of bases, held together by hydrogen bonds between pairs of identical bases, turned out to be incorrect, for several reasons. One problem with this structure was that the backbones of such a two-chain DNA molecule would buckle in and out because of the different shapes of the bases. Another problem, as Crick had pointed out, was that Watson's proposed structure would not explain the Chargaff ratio of bases for DNA.

The solution to both problems came quickly. On Saturday morning, February 28, Watson wrote later, he was shifting his cardboard models about on his desk. "Suddenly I became aware that an adenine-thymine pair held together by two hydrogen bonds was identical in shape to a guanine-

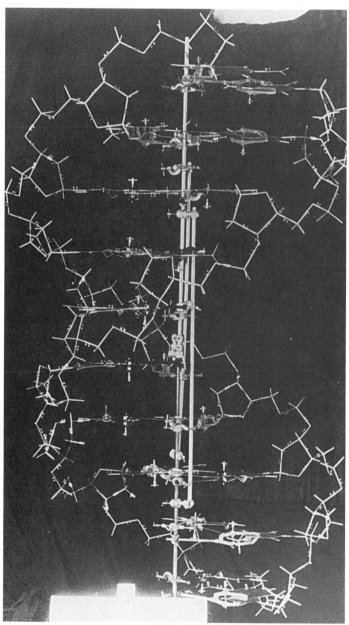

The original demonstration model of the double helix that was constructed by Watson and Crick.

cytosine pair held together by at least two hydrogen bonds," he wrote. "All the hydrogen bonds seemed to form natural-ly; no fudging was required to make the two types of base pairs identical in shape."

When Crick came in and heard the news, he saw immediately that Watson's discovery would satisfy the requirements of the Chargaff ratio. He also made a crucial discovery—that the way the bases would attach to their phosphates meant that the sequence of bases in the two backbones would have to run in opposite directions. "That was the crucial fact," Crick said years later. "The chains must come in pairs rather than three in a molecule, and one chain must run down and the other up."

Jerry Donohue, a young American student working with Watson, added one crucial idea. It was already known that bases come in two forms known collectively as tau-tomers, one called keto and the other enol. The difference between them is the location of just one hydrogen atom, but that is enough to change the size of the base. In Watson's original model, the bases had the enol form. Donohue told Watson about new scientific evidence that the bases were much more likely to have the keto form. That information solidified the case for adenine-purine base binding in the DNA molecule. Having the bases in the keto form means that the cytosine-guanine bond is triple while the thymine-adenine bond is double, so that the pairs always match correctly.

Now Watson and Crick had their model: two DNA chains, coiled as alpha helixes 20 angstrom units in diame-ter, making a complete turn every 34 angstrom units, with the bases in each chain 3.4 angstrom units apart. This struc-ture can be pictured as a railroad track with the phosphate chains making up the tracks and the bases as the ties between the tracks. This two-chain structure would coil to the right around an imaginary center line.

This was a model that allowed the DNA molecule to

reproduce itself. The two chains could separate, which would allow each purine to pair with the appropriate pyrimidine, to produce two new chains identical with the original ones.

As far as it went, this was a good idea, but Watson and Crick knew they would not be home free until they could build a complete model that satisfied all the chemical and structural requirements. Nevertheless, Crick went to his favorite pub that afternoon "to tell everyone within hearing distance that we had found the secret of life." Crick eventually named his family's house in Cambridge the Golden Helix and put a brass helix on the front of it.

As for Watson, he recalled later that "it seemed almost unbelievable that the DNA structure was solved, that the answer was incredibly exciting, and that our names would be associated with the double helix as Pauling's was with the alpha helix."

Years later, Watson was asked to give a talk to a small, exclusive club of scientists at Cambridge. After having a few drinks, he gave his talk coherently until the very end, when he came to sum up. All he was able to say about the model was, "It's so beautiful, you see, so beautiful."

That was in the future. First the news about the double helix's structure had to be illustrated and circulated. As Watson and Crick waited impatiently, the Cambridge machine shop began to produce the precise molecular models of all the DNA components they needed. By March 7, they had built a complete model, standing more than six feet tall, of their DNA molecule.

Maurice Wilkins saw the model and liked it. Linus Pauling, who had been told about the proposed structure in a letter from a scientific associate, visited Cambridge the first week in April, saw the model, and agreed that the structure looked right. The Watson and Crick paper describing the structure was sent off to the journal *Nature* on April 2 and appeared on April 25. It included one par-

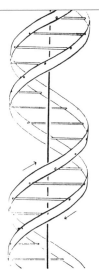

This figure is purely diagrammatic. The two ribbons symbolize the two phosphate—sugar chains, and the horizontal rods the pairs of bases holding the chains together. The vertical line marks the fibre axis

This page from the 1953 Nature *magazine article shows the double helix as Watson and Crick first described it.*

chain, so that the structure repeats after 10 residues on each chain, that is, after 34 A. The distance of a phosphorus atom from the fibre axis is 10 A. As the phosphates are on the outside, cations have easy access to them.

The structure is an open one, and its water content is rather high. At lower water contents we would expect the bases to tilt so that the structure could become more compact.

The novel feature of the structure is the manner in which the two chains are held together by the purine and pyrimidine bases. The planes of the bases are perpendicular to the fibre axis. They are joined together in pairs, a single base from one chain being hydrogen-bonded to a single base from the other chain, so that the two lie side by side with identical z-co-ordinates. One of the pair must be a purine and the other a pyrimidine for bonding to occur. The hydrogen bonds are made as follows : purine position 1 to pyrimidine position 1 ; purine position 6 to pyrimidine position 6.

If it is assumed that the bases only occur in the structure in the most plausible tautomeric forms

2

ticularly important sentence, which read, "It has not escaped our notice that the specific pairing we have postulated immediately suggests a possible copying mechanism for the genetic material."

The paper had an immense impact, Crick wrote on the 25th anniversary of its publication. Many scientists believed that if it had not been Watson and Crick who had made the discovery in the way they did, he said, "Instead of being revealed with a flourish it would have trickled out and its impact would have been far less."

And, he added, "Rather than believe that Watson and Crick made the DNA structure, I would stress that the structure made Watson and Crick. After all, I was almost totally unknown at the time and Watson was regarded, in most circles, as too bright to be really sound."

One striking example of how their discovery changed their lives was the interest that certain Hollywood studios expressed in doing a full-length Watson-Crick movie. Any movie would necessarily have a great set of characters, Crick realized—the brash young American, the Englishman who talked too much "and who therefore must be a genius since geniuses either talk all the time or say nothing at all . . . and best of all, a Liberated Woman [Rosalind Franklin] who appears to be unfairly treated." Southern California was the home of the movie industry, and several studios there expressed interest in making a film about the discovery of the double helix. Jim Watson wanted a movie. Francis Crick opposed the idea at first, but changed his mind later. Friends advised them to draw up a contract to cover all the possibilities, including the sharing of profits from a possible musical comedy and comic book rights. Watson and Crick even hired an agent and a Hollywood lawyer. But Crick predicted that a movie would never be made—because the story did not have enough sex and violence, he said.

Crick's prediction proved accurate, at least as far as a Hollywood movie was concerned. The British Broadcasting Corporation did make a docudrama in the late 1980s. Crick was played by Tim Piggott, Watson by Jeff Goldblum. The

program was shown in the United States under the title *Double Helix*. One failing of the docudrama, Crick said later, was that it did not show "that the double helix was not an ending but a beginning, because of all the ideas it suggested about gene replication, protein synthesis, and so on"—ideas that were among the ones Crick pursued in his later work.

Watson (left) and Crick at the 1953 announcement of their discovery of DNA's molecular structure.

In a second paper that was published a few weeks after the one describing DNA structure, Watson and Crick outlined some of the implications of their finding. "Any sequence of the pairs of bases can fit into the structure," they wrote. "It follows that in a long molecule many different permutations are possible, and it therefore seems likely that the precise sequence of the bases is the code which carries the genetical information. If the actual order of the bases on one of the pairs of chains were given, one could write down the exact order of the bases on the other one, because of the specific pairing."

And they also wrote a paper explaining one of the crucial central features of genetics: the fact that mutations can appear. These mutations, or changes in DNA, can cause genetic diseases. But they are also involved in the process of evolution, including the appearance of new species. "Spontaneous mutation may be due to a base occasionally occurring in one of its less likely tautomeric forms," they wrote. For example, while adenine normally pairs with thymine, a shift of a single hydrogen atom would enable it to pair with guanine, creating a variant DNA chain. That was only speculation when it was first written, but it was proved to be true within a few years.

Watson and Crick also noted a problem about DNA structure that had to be solved: "Since the two chains in our model are intertwined, it is essential for them to untwist if they are to separate. . . . A considerable amount of uncoiling would be necessary," they wrote. "Although it is difficult at the moment to see how these processes occur without everything getting tangled, we do not feel that this objection will be insuperable."

Not long after that paper and several others were published, Watson and Crick went off in different directions. Crick received a fellowship from Brooklyn Polytechnic Institute in New York. He had some doubts about going to Brooklyn (which became the subject of many jokes), but his curiosity to see the United States led him to accept the offer. Watson went to the California Institute of Technology, which had offered him a position. They never again worked together at the same institution. Yet they continued to collaborate, writing frequently to each other and getting together at scientific meetings, and they continued to have a major role in the development of the new genetics.

The first independent confirmation of their proposed structure for DNA came from Rosalind Franklin, who published a paper saying that the Watson–Crick structure fit her X-ray diffraction studies of both Type A and Type B DNA. Many other studies were then done that also confirmed their findings. The scientific world soon agreed that the problem of DNA structure had been solved.

6

How DNA Works

While the Watson-Crick paper of 1953 solved the riddle of DNA structure, it did not say anything about how genetic information was carried by that structure or how the information in DNA was transferred to cells to make proteins. Solving those riddles would take several more years, although general ideas about them had begun to emerge.

Even before the structure of DNA was described, Watson already had a good idea of how DNA information was transferred to cells—by governing the production of RNA molecules that then produced proteins. "Virtually all the evidence then available made me believe that DNA was the template upon which RNA chains were made," he wrote later. "In turn, RNA chains were the likely candidates for the templates for protein synthesis. . . . On the wall above my desk I taped up a paper sheet saying DNA ➤ RNA ➤ protein. The arrows did not signify chemical transformations, but instead expressed the transfer of genetic information from the sequences of nucleotides in DNA molecules to the sequences of amino acids in proteins."

In one of their follow-up papers Watson and Crick said that "the precise sequence of the bases is the code which

Watson and Crick pose with fellow scientists in the 1960s. They called themselves the "RNA Tie Club" and wore ties patterned with an image of an RNA strand.

carries the genetical information." This idea came from Crick, who made two then-daring assumptions. One was that the sequence of nucleotides in DNA, and nothing else, determined the order of amino acids in a protein. An even more daring assumption was that no further information other than what was carried in the DNA molecule was needed to build a protein: Once the information from DNA was translated so that a string of amino acids could be put together, that string—a protein—would fold into its biologically active three-dimensional form. But Watson and Crick noted that the way information was transferred from DNA to make proteins was still unknown.

They soon got a letter from George Gamow, a theoretical physicist in the United States, who had a novel idea to propose. Gamow is known for his work on the nuclear reactions that power a star, the joining together of hydrogen atoms to release energy in vast amounts, and the later reactions that create the more complex elements. Writing about DNA, Gamow suggested that the sequence of bases in a DNA molecule formed diamond-shaped holes of slightly different shapes. If this were so, Gamow proposed, individual amino acids could fit into specific holes in the DNA molecule the way that keys fit into locks, eventually coming together to form a protein chain.

Gamow's idea was wrong, but it showed how Watson and Crick had captured the interest of scientists. And it had one beneficial effect. Gamow's idea inspired Crick to write out his ideas about the way DNA carried the information that led to protein formation. The fundamental problem with Gamow's scheme, he wrote, is that "it does not distinguish between the direction of a sequence. . . . There is little doubt that Nature makes this distinction."

But Gamow was correct in one of his proposals. He put down a list of amino acids, in the order of their abundance in nature, and drew a line after the first 20. Watson and Crick, meanwhile, were making their own list of a standard set of amino acids of which natural proteins are composed. Their list left out amino acids that were found in only a few odd proteins. Like Gamow's list, theirs had 20 entries, which turned out not only to be correct but also to be virtually identical with Gamow's list.

The number 20 proved to be a significant one, because it set a lower limit on the number of bases needed to code for an amino acid. There are four bases in DNA, so a combination of two can code for only 4 x 4 = 16 amino acids. Three bases, or 4 x 4 x 4 = 64, can code for all of the 20 amino acids, with room left over. But that still left the question of the exact nature of a three-base code. Was it an overlapping code, so that each amino acid was determined by two bases and the preceding base (the first three bases coded one amino acid, then bases 3, 4, and 5 coded the next base, bases 4, 5, and 6 coded the next base, and so on), or was a fixed sequence of three bases required, so that bases 1, 2, and 3 coded for one amino acid, bases 4, 5, and 6 coded for the next, and so on?

The way DNA duplicates itself soon became clear. It begins with the two strands of the double helix unwinding. Then the weak bonds between base pairs are broken and two new complementary chains are made. In humans and other higher organisms, this process of DNA replication, as it is called, takes place in the cell nucleus.

At least as important was the question of how the information carried in the double helix is translated into an amino acid. The eventual answer came out of work begun more than a decade earlier, when scientists began looking at the interior of cells with the electron microscope.

An electron microscope creates an image by shooting a stream of electrons through whatever is being studied. It can pick out extremely small details inside a cell, but a good deal of skill is needed to prepare a specimen that can show those details. An extremely thin slice of the cell must be cut and then covered with a thin film of metal atoms, which will produce an image when bombarded with electrons from the microscope.

When scientists such as Albert Claude and George Palade of the Rockefeller Institute in New York began examining these samples, they saw that the cytoplasm of a cell, the part outside the nucleus, was filled with a network of connected channels, filaments, and tubules. This network was soon named the "endoplasmic reticulum," a phrase meaning "the network inside the cell." A large number of small, dense, spherical particles about 150 angstrom units in diameter were seen in the endoplasmic reticulum. When they were spun in a centrifuge, these particles, which were given the name of ribosomes, were found to contain RNA and protein.

Biologist Albert Claude's work on the cell contributed to the discovery of endoplasmic reticulum, a system of membranes responsible for transporting materials within the cell.

In 1953, a team led by Paul Zamecnik at Massachusetts General Hospital showed that the ribosomes were the site where amino acids were put together to make proteins. Zamecnik's team went on to develop a system that could make proteins outside a cell. This system contained 24 amino acids and ribosomes. It also contained what was then called soluble RNA, molecules of RNA that floated in the fluid of the cytoplasm. The system also included some enzymes that the scientists had isolated from cells, and a molecule called adenosine triphosphate, or ATP, which had been identified as the source of energy for protein synthesis. ATP consists of an adenine to which three phosphate groups are attached. The bonds holding the phosphates are easily broken, and when they are they release a large amount of energy that can power molecular reactions. It was not clear to the Zamecnik group exactly how their protein-making system worked, but it did.

Francis Crick supplied a possible answer in the summer of 1954 on a visit to the United States. He proposed that there was a yet-undiscovered family of molecules, which he called adaptors, each of which had two active ends. One end of a molecule would attach itself to a specific amino acid. The other end would attach itself to a place on the DNA molecule that carried the base sequence for that particular amino acid. The amino acids would thus be brought together along the DNA chain in the proper sequence that would enable them to join together to form a protein. The adaptor molecules that carried the amino acids could well be made of nucleic acids, Crick thought.

An adaptor molecule had to have very specific characteristics, Crick said. To begin with, it had to be able to identify its correct amino acid. Then it had to find the location on the strand of DNA where the genetic code called for that amino acid to be attached. Finally, it had to attach its amino acid to a growing protein chain, then go off to find another amino acid. There could very well be more than one adaptor for each amino acid, he suggested.

"The adaptor hypothesis implies that the actual set of twenty amino acids found in proteins is either due to a historical accident or to biological selection at an extremely early stage," he wrote. "This is not impossible, since once the twenty had been fixed it would be very difficult to make a change without altering every protein in the organism, a change which almost certainly would be lethal."

Crick already had a good idea of what an adaptor would have to be made of. He believed that adaptors were RNA molecules. "I have tacitly dealt with DNA throughout," Crick wrote in one of his papers, "but the argument would carry over to some types of RNA structure. . . . Base pairing may be absent in RNA or take a radically different form. . . .

Robert Holley examines a strip of tape representing RNA. Holley and his coworkers were the first scientists to determine the structure and sequence of RNA.

Without a structure for RNA one can only guess."

Determining the structure of the RNA molecules found in cells proved to be a difficult task. RNA could not be crystallized, so creating a diffraction pattern for it was impossible. And there were several kinds of RNA, some single stranded and others double stranded, to be found in a single cell.

The structure of one kind of RNA that acted as an adaptor was first described by Robert Holley, who led a research team at Cornell University in Ithaca, New York. Holley built on the work of Paul Berg, who purified many of the soluble RNAs and showed that different RNAs that acted as adaptors carried different amino acids. These molecules today are no longer called adaptors but "transfer RNA," abbreviated tRNA.

In a project that lasted seven years, Holley purified a small amount of transfer RNA that was specific for the amino acid alanine and established that it had 77 nucleotides. Holley then determined the sequence of the alanine tRNA—the first time a sequence of any RNA had been identified—and showed that it had a cloverleaf form. The alanine molecule was attached to one arm of the cloverleaf. At the other end of the tRNA were three nucleotides that attached themselves to the appropriate sequence of nucleotides on the DNA molecule. He discovered that there is a different transfer RNA for each amino acid. The individual tRNAs pick up the amino acids and transfer them to the ribosome, where the chain of amino acids is put together to form a protein. Holley won a share of the Nobel Prize for his work in this area.

Francis Crick did some of the crucial work to establish that the genetic code consisted of base triplets: a sequence of three bases in the DNA molecule coded for an amino acid, for a stop, or for a start signal. Working at Cambridge, Crick and an associate, Sidney Brenner, did a long series of complex experiments in which they induced mutations in

DNA, changing individual bases in the DNA chain of phage viruses and seeing how those mutations affected the ability of phage to infect bacteria.

The key experiment was one in which they induced triple mutations in phage DNA. They then added the mutated phage viruses to petri dishes on which a thin film of bacteria was growing. If a mutated phage virus demonstrated an ability to infect the bacteria, the result would be a plaque—a small area in the petri dish that was clear, because the bacteria in that area had been killed by the phage. Generally, the mutations killed the infective ability of the phage.

The climax of the experiment occurred one evening, when Crick returned to the laboratory after dinner with a colleague, Leslie Barnett, to inspect the petri dishes. "One glance at the crucial plate was sufficient," Crick recalled years later. "There were plaques in it. The triple mutant was showing the wild-type behavior." After carefully checking the plate to be sure that all was correct, Crick turned to Barnett and said, "Do you realize that you and I are the only people in the world who know it's a triple code?"

The two men had worked with three distinct mutants. Each mutant had a single mutation that was enough to knock out the function of the phage gene. Yet if they put all three mutations together in the same gene, that gene started to work again. The combination of two or four mutations did not have the same result, however. The gene began to work again only if three mutations were combined. This could happen, Crick argued, only if the code were a triplet code. When the results of the experiment were published soon afterward in a scientific journal, the world knew that the genetic code was a triple one.

Since then, the genetic code has been completely worked out. Each triplet of DNA nucleotides is called a codon. There are 64 codons, which code for just 20 amino acids. Other unusual amino acids can appear in some proteins, but they are made by chemical changes to one of the

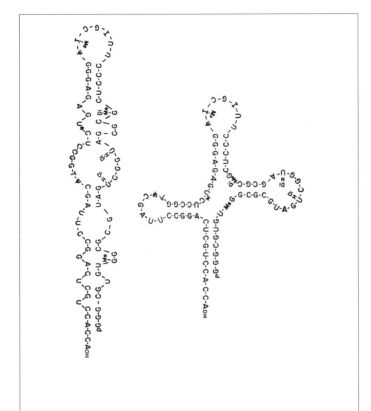

This page from Holley's notes diagrams his proposed arrangements of the RNA chain with its double-stranded regions.

Fig. 6. Two hypothetical arrangements of the RNA chain with double-stranded regions.

20 original amino acids. There is a lot of duplication in the code. For example, UUU specifies the amino acid phenylalanine, but so does UUC. Valine has four different codons; leucine has six. Three codons—UAA, UAG, and UGA—each specify the end of a protein. There is no codon to signal the start of a protein chain.

Crick played an important role in establishing the genetic terminology that scientists now use. But one word he did not establish was *code,* which was already in widespread use. To an expert in linguistics, *code* is not the appropriate word for genetics, because a code is a system in which each word stands for a corresponding word. *Cipher* is the right word, because cipher translates letter by letter, so that only a small key is needed. This is a common mistake in language, though—like the genetic code, Morse code is actually a cipher, not a code.

Knowing the genetic code explains many features of life, ranging from genetic disease to evolution. The key is mutation—a change in a single codon that causes a different amino acid to be put into the protein chain. Most mutations are either neutral or harmful. A few—and only a very few—are beneficial. Over a long period, beneficial mutations can accumulate until finally a new organism emerges. When Darwin proposed the theory of evolution, one criticism of it was that the mechanism by which organisms evolved was then unknown. Genetics has since provided the mechanism that underlies evolution: the changes in DNA that are translated into changes in proteins.

One question that still had to be answered was whether ribosomes carried in their RNA the information needed to put together proteins. Several studies pointed in a different direction. First, ribosomal RNA was found to come in just two sizes, not the large number of sizes that would be needed to carry the necessary information. Second, the base composition of ribosomal RNA varied very little compared to the base composition of DNA. The RNA of a ribosome did not have the information-carrying variety found of DNA. Until 1960, it was believed that ribosomal RNA (rRNA) molecules could serve as templates on which proteins could be synthesized, but that was just a hypothesis.

The ribosome issue was settled by a project that has become known as the PaJaMo experiment, because it was done by Arthur Pardee, an American, and two French biologists, François Jacob and Jacques Monod, who worked at the Institut Pasteur in Paris. They looked at the activity of an enzyme called beta-galactosidase, which is produced when a cell is given the sugar galactose (which is different from glucose, ordinary table sugar). They found that cells immediately produced this enzyme when exposed to the unusual sugar—something that would be impossible if the ribosome carried the message for the production of that and all other enzymes, because it would take some time for the ribosome to adjust to producing that particular enzyme.

The PaJaMo experiment showed that RNA does serve as a template, but it is not the RNA of the ribosomes. Instead, it was found that small RNA molecules now called messenger RNA, or mRNA, carry the information of the genes to the ribosomes in the cell cytoplasm. The ribosomes move along the mRNA, translating its information into the sequence of amino acids that make up a protein. Ribosomes thus are not specific for any protein. Instead they serve as factories for translating genetic information into protein production.

Crick heard about the PaJaMo experiment from Jacques Monod at a party. He later described that moment as "a sudden flash of enlightenment" that he would never forget. This experiment cleared away a number of difficulties about protein production. "I woke up that morning with only a set of confused ideas about the overall control of protein synthesis," Crick later wrote. "When I went to bed all our difficulties had resolved and the shining answers stood clear before us." But he added that it would take "months and years of work" to identify all the molecules involved in protein synthesis.

One of those molecules was identified by work on phages, the viruses that infect bacteria. Experiments showed that when phage viruses enter bacteria, a certain kind of RNA is quickly produced in large quantities. These RNA molecules have a base structure that mirrors the structure of the DNA of the infecting phage virus. In other words, this is a form of RNA that carries the information contained in the phage DNA to a ribosome, where transfer RNA can use that information to build proteins. The RNA that carries the message from DNA is called messenger RNA, abbreviated mRNA.

There still were many uncertainties about the relationship between nucleic acids and proteins. Crick took a major step toward clarifying the situation in a lecture he delivered in 1957. In it he made two proposals, one he called the Sequence Hypothesis, the other the Central Dogma.

The Sequence Hypothesis, as Crick explained it, was that "the specificity of a piece of nucleic acid is expressed solely by the sequence of its bases, and this sequence is a (simple) code for the amino acid sequence of a particular protein." He added that the way a protein folded up to assume its three-dimensional shape "is simply a function of the order of amino acids."

As Crick described it, the Sequence Hypothesis "unites several remarkable pairs of generalizations." For example, it asserts that proteins have a central importance for the biochemical reactions that occur in living things. They are the molecules that carry out the everyday business of cells and are the bodies of which cells are made: for digestion, waste disposal, and so on. The genes, on the other hand, have a dominating biological role. They are the molecules that ultimately govern the proteins and are responsible for transmitting all the traits of living beings from generation to generation. And all the information needed for these vital functions is contained in the sequence of the bases that make up the nucleic acid of a gene.

The Central Dogma that Crick laid out said that "once 'information' has passed into protein it cannot get out again. In more detail, the transfer of information from nucleic acid to nucleic acid, or from nucleic acid to protein may be possible, but transfer from protein to protein, or from protein to nucleic acid is impossible."

The Central Dogma is a simple, short statement, but it is as important for biology and genetics as Albert Einstein's formula $E = mc^2$ is for physics. One reason is that it explains why the characteristics that an organism acquires in life, but not from its genes, cannot be inherited by its offspring. For example, a man can work hard to build up his muscles, but those big muscles will not be passed along to a son or daughter, because they are not part of the body's genetic information. If the children want their own big muscles, they will have to work for them the way their father did. On the other hand, hair color is a trait that is passed on to children, since it is governed by the genes.

Both of the ideas proposed by Crick are accepted today as basic tenets of molecular biology, but they were somewhat controversial at that time. For example, Barry Commoner, a scientist who became famous not so much for his scientific work as for his opposition to nuclear testing, wrote at the time that DNA could not be "the master molecule" that duplicated itself and carried the information needed to make proteins. It could not be that simple, Commoner maintained. The unit of duplication, he argued, "is not DNA but a multi-molecular system which is so complex as to require the participation of the entire living cell."

Crick acknowledged that because his Central Dogma was a negative statement, it was hard to prove. But as he later wrote, transmitting information from DNA to proteins required very complex machinery. "It seemed unlikely on general grounds that this machinery could easily work backwards," he noted. "The only reasonable alternative was that the cell had evolved an entirely separate set of complicated machinery for back translation, and of this there was no trace, and no reason to believe that it might be needed."

Crick was right and Commoner and the other critics wrong. Both the Sequence Hypothesis and the Central Dogma are today accepted as basic principles of genetics.

Several surprising characteristics of the DNA that makes up human genes have emerged over the years. One is that a stretch of DNA that codes for a peptide chain is not necessarily continuous but can be interrupted by long stretches of DNA that do not carry coding information.

These segments are called introns; the segments that carry information are called exons. The introns are eliminated from messenger RNA by a process known as splicing.

"The existence of introns came as almost a complete surprise," Crick wrote. "Nobody had clearly postulated their existence before experimenters stumbled on them by accident. . . . There was no hint of them from classical genetics, even in an organism such as yeast on which relatively high resolution genetic mapping had been carried out."

Introns are found mainly in higher organisms, including humans. In humans, the intron sequences are often longer than the information-carrying exons. But in primitive organisms like bacteria there are few or no introns.

It has also been discovered that most of the DNA in human cells—perhaps as much as 90 percent—appears to be meaningless. In an article Crick suggested that this "selfish DNA," as he called it, might have originated as DNA parasites that jumped from place to place on a chromosome, leaving replicas of themselves behind. In time, Crick proposed, many of these sequences would be rendered meaningless by random mutations. This is a fascinating theory, but no one has yet discovered why these meaningless runs of DNA make up so much of human DNA or whether they have some function that may someday be detected.

Crick left Cambridge in 1977 and went to the United States. Several years before, he had been a nonresident fellow of the Salk Institute for Biological Studies in La Jolla, California, just north of San Diego. It was named for Jonas Salk, the inventor of the cure for poliomyelitis. There Crick became a permanent member of the Salk Institute's staff and a professor in the biochemistry department of the University of California, San Diego.

His reason for joining Salk, Crick explained later, was that he had decided to study the workings of the brain. "I realized that if I were ever to study the brain more closely it was now or never, since I had just passed 60."

Francis Crick, at the Salk Institute for Biological Sciences in La Jolla, California, where he served as president from 1994 to 1995.

There, like so many others he liked the weather. "Personally, I feel at home in Southern California," Crick explained. "I like the prosperity and the relaxed way of life. The easy access to the ocean, the mountains and the desert is also an attraction. There are miles of lovely beaches to walk on—out of season they are usually almost deserted." But he confessed that he felt "much less at home in the rest of America."

While enjoying the climate, Crick also went hard to work. The topic he chose was vision and how the brain handled it—a subject he acknowledged that he knew nothing about. His appointment in psychology at the University of California came about when he began seeking information from scientists in that department. He continued to do work on DNA, though, and in addition was named president of the Salk Institute in 1994.

Crick also pursued more speculative ideas that raised some eyebrows. With a fellow scientist, Leslie Orgel, Crick proposed a theory of "directed panspermia," which said that life on earth had perhaps originated from microorganisms sent to this planet on a spaceship from a higher civilization. Two facts led to this theory, Crick said. One was the uniformity of the genetic code, which suggested that at some early stage life had evolved through a population bottleneck. The other was that the life of the universe has been calculated to be twice the age of the earth, based on the abundance of various elements in the stars and galaxies, which would have allowed advanced civilizations to evolve elsewhere before living things appeared on earth.

Directed panspermia was in fact only a semiserious proposal. On the more substantial side, Crick began to study the brain and the mechanisms of consciousness, about which very little was known. Crick told researchers at one meeting that in a decade or two researchers in psychology departments would be working on "molecular psychology."

To support this suggestion, Crick argued that "if you don't accept that, look at what has happened to biology departments. Nowadays most of the scientists there are doing molecular biology, whereas a generation ago that was a subject known only to specialists."

One DNA-related enterprise that Crick did not involve himself in was the Human Genome Project, the government-sponsored effort to create a complete map and sequence of all the human chromosomes. It was instead Jim Watson who soon began to play an important role in that project.

Francis Crick has not been as much in the limelight as Jim Watson in recent years, but his career has continued to be productive, and controversial in several ways. He remains at the Salk Institute for Biological Studies, where he served as president in 1994 and 1995, appreciating the relaxed southern California way of life.

Despite that atmosphere and his many honors—the list could cover several pages—Crick has continued to do research, and to affect how other scientists do research. As one biographer said of him, "By brain, wit, vigor of personality, strength of voice, intellectual charm and scorn, a lot of travel and ceaseless letter-writing, Crick coordinated the research of many other biologists, disciplined their thinking, arbitrated their conflicts, communicated and explained their results. As he went, he sorted the important from the less important with a brisk efficiency that now serves well to distinguish the main line of molecular biology from all else that was in biochemistry."

In large part because of Crick's interests, the focus of the Salk Institute has changed since he went there. At first, researchers at the institute were doing little or no work in neuroscience, the focus of Crick's attention. Over the years, however, the institute has recruited a large number of neuroscientists, so that now a substantial part of the institute's research is focused on the workings of the brain.

One thing Crick discovered was that "although much is known about the behavior of the neurons in many parts of the visual system (at least in monkeys), nobody really has any clear idea how we see anything at all. This unhappy fact is never mentioned to students of the subject. Neurophysiologists have some glimpses into how the brain takes the picture apart, how somewhat separate areas of our cerebral cortex process motion, color, shape, position in space, and so on. What is not yet understood is how the brain puts all this together to give us our vivid unitary picture of the world." Francis Crick is working to unravel this mystery.

Sickle-cell anemia is a genetic disease in which hemoglobin, the oxygen-carrying molecule of the red blood cells, is seriously deformed, giving the cells a sickled, abnormally curved appearance. The cells become fragile and easily destroyed, and cannot pass through the smallest blood vessels. Sickle-cell anemia occurs when a child inherits two genes for this abnormality. The incidence of sickle-cell anemia is highest in African Americans, because those who carry one mutated gene have developed an increased resistance to the life-threatening malaria that can be common in Africa.

When molecular biology techniques became available, the first studies of hemoglobin found no difference between the amino acid composition of the normal molecule and the hemoglobin of sickle-cell patients. But hemoglobin is a large molecule consisting of four interlocking protein chains, so a mutation was not easy to detect. The mutation was eventually discovered by the biochemist Vernon Ingram, working at Harvard University in the 1950s.

Ingram first used an enzyme to break up the protein chains of normal and sickle-cell hemoglobin into short pieces. Then he looked for differences between the pieces. First he boiled the samples to open up the protein chains. Then he broke down the samples into even smaller pieces by exposing them to a digestive enzyme, trypsin, which breaks protein bonds at known locations. The next step was to place drops of each sample on specially treated wet filter paper and expose the paper to an electric current for more than two hours, knowing that different pieces of protein would migrate across the paper at varying rates.

The protein fragments appeared as irregular blobs on the filter paper. Looking closely, Ingram detected a difference between the blob patterns of the normal and sickle-cell samples—one sickle-cell blob was different from the matching normal blob. He had located the segment of protein that was mutated in sickle-cell anemia.

The next step was to identify the exact difference. Sequencing the two differing segments, Ingram found the difference: In sickle-cell hemoglobin, a glutamic acid amino acid found in the normal chain is replaced by a valine. This difference alone is enough to distort the entire hemoglobin molecule.

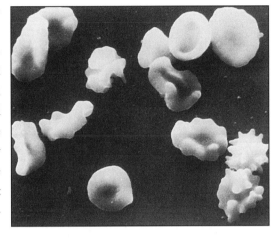

Ingram's discovery made it possible to test for sickle-cell anemia before birth.

Both normal red blood cells (center foreground and upper right) and deformed cells (upper left and lower right) can be seen in this sample of blood taken from a person with sickle-cell anemia.

When both parents are known each to carry one sickle-cell gene, the unborn baby can be tested to determine whether it has two sickle-cell genes and thus will have the disease at birth. Similar techniques are being used for the prenatal detection of other recessive genetic conditions.

Watson and the Human Genome Project

After the double helix achievement, Jim Watson left England, returning to the United States. Three years later he went to Harvard University, where he soon became a full professor. In 1968 he moved to the Cold Spring Harbor Laboratory of Quantitative Biology, located on the north shore of Long Island in New York.

Both at Harvard and at Cold Spring Harbor, Watson produced impressive results—not only in the research he did but in the younger scientists he trained. A stream of notable work came out of his laboratory, and he trained a cadre of new scientists who had—and have—warm memories of him. They and most other scientists paid less attention to the wise-guy attitude of *The Double Helix,* his book about the discovery of DNA, than to another book he wrote, *The Molecular Biology of the Gene,* a textbook that made a lasting impression on molecular biologists all over the world. Francis Crick was one of many who noted that the real-life Jim Watson was very different from the swash-

Alfred Hershey (left) and James Watson sailing at Cold Spring Harbor, Long Island, in the 1960s. Hershey and a colleague, Martha Chase, showed that DNA is the genetic material for viruses.

buckling picture he painted of himself in *The Double Helix*.

Watson soon was named director of Cold Spring Harbor and proceeded to build the laboratory into one of national significance, attracting talented young scientists and substantial increases in grant money for pioneering experimental work. The world soon noticed that Watson's achievements after the discovery of DNA remained impressive. In 1962, for example, he was one of only two biologists listed by *Life* magazine among the 100 most important men and women in the United States. And in 1990 Watson and Jonas Salk were the only biologists to be included in *Life's* roster of the 100 most important Americans of the 20th century.

In 1988, at the age of 61, Jim Watson took on the post of director of the Human Genome Project at the National Institutes of Health (NIH). This federally funded effort had the goal of identifying and mapping every gene in the human body and finding the sequence of all the bases in human DNA. It was a part-time job for Watson, who remained director of the Cold Spring Harbor Laboratory and commuted to the genome job two or three days a week. The genome project was just then getting started and did not get significant funding until 1991. Watson's agreement to head the project was regarded by scientists as showing the program's critics that it had scientific validity. Norton Zinder, who headed the NIH advisory committee on the program, said that Watson's agreement to serve made "a quantum leap in the program's credibility."

There were, however, many critics who feared that the genome program would turn out to be a major government invasion of individuals' genetic privacy. One national magazine, *The New Republic,* ran a highly critical story and put Watson's picture on its cover over the caption "Mad Scientist?"

Watson won a great deal of praise for getting the project off to a good start, but a clash of personalities forced him out after four years.

The idea for the Human Genome Project originated in 1985 when Robert Sinsheimer, chancellor of the University of California at Santa Cruz, called a group of scientists together to consider the idea of analyzing large-scale sequencing. Most of the scientists were skeptical at first, for several reasons. One was that since about 90 percent of the human genome does not code for genes, constructing a complete sequence would not tell us much. Another objection was that any huge, highly coordinated program would distort the tradition of independent scientific research. Nevertheless, after a series of meetings held over several years, the idea of the genome project was approved.

It was the U.S. Department of Energy that took the first step. The Energy Department owns the four big national laboratories that have evolved from the atomic bomb project of World War II. These facilities had a large cadre of biologists who had been studying the genetic mutations caused by radiation, so they were already sequencing stretches of DNA. The Energy Department was also looking for a new scientific project that would increase its funding. The agency began its human genome effort in the mid-1980s.

The National Institutes of Health soon became involved. In 1987 James B. Wyngaarden, director of the NIH, set up a special Office of Human Genome Research to advise on a human genome mapping effort. The next year, the Department of Energy and the NIH signed an agreement to coordinate their genome efforts. The target date of 2005 has been set for completion of the project.

Jim Watson seemed to be a natural choice to head the genome program, but he had his doubts. "I felt uneasy when I heard rumors that I was to be offered the position," Watson wrote later. "My job at Cold Spring Harbor was already more than full time. If I ran the genome effort, I would hold two demanding positions simultaneously. Yet, if

I turned down the job, it was not clear that any prominent scientist still active in the lab would take on the task. So when Wyngaarden asked me to come to Bethesda [Maryland] to talk about working for NIH, I knew I would accept. By then I realized that only once would I have the opportunity to let my scientific life encompass the path from double helix to the 3 billion steps of the human genome."

The possibility of being able to discover the complete set of human genetic instructions "seemed an undreamable scientific objective in 1953 when Francis Crick and I found the double helical structure of DNA," Watson said. But he was clear that "a more important set of instruction books will never be found by human beings. When finally interpreted, the genetic messages encoded within our DNA molecules will provide the ultimate answers to the chemical underpinnings of human existence. They will not only help us understand how we function as healthy human beings, but will also explain, at the chemical level, the role of genetic factors in a multitude of diseases, such as cancer, Alzheimer's disease, and schizophrenia, that diminish the individual lives of so many millions of people."

The Human Genome Project is an awesome effort. As Watson noted, there are about 3 billion bases in the human genome, and anywhere from 50,000 to 100,000 genes in human cells. When the project began, some 5,000 human genes had been identified, but only about 1,900 of them had been mapped to chromosomes. Genes make up only about 2 percent of the entire genome. Some non-gene DNA helps genes to function in various ways, but the rest of it is useless.

One central effort of the genome project is DNA sequencing. The first methods for sequencing DNA were developed in the 1970s. They were slow and expensive, costing more than $5 a base pair. By the mid-1990s, though, several laboratories had developed automated methods that enabled them to sequence more than 1 million base pairs per year. The cost had come down to 50 cents a base pair, and it was heading even lower.

Along with sequencing goes genetic mapping, the location of specific genes on specific chromosomes. One way to map a gene is based on the knowledge that when a cell divides and the strands of DNA in its chromosomes separate so they can duplicate themselves, the separation is sometimes flawed. The threads of DNA keep breaking and recombining with other threads. One way to tell how close two genes are to each other on the genetic map is to study how often they are separated by this kind of recombination.

A newer way to map genes makes use of restriction enzymes, which cut DNA strands at specific base sequences. Restriction enzymes are obtained from bacteria, which use them as defenses against invading viruses. Scientists have isolated a number of restriction enzymes to use in experiments.

The value of restriction enzymes in gene mapping is based on the recognition that human DNA sequences vary widely from person to person. If a chromosome is exposed to a restriction enzyme, the result is a bunch of fragments called RFLPs (pronounced *riflips),* short for "restriction fragment length polymorphisms." Because of the differences in human chromosomes, individuals each provide their own unique RFLP sequences.

One way to use RFLPs is to test members of a large family, some of whose members have a genetic disease while others do not. It is possible to find a specific riflip pattern in family members who have the genetic disease, but not in disease-free relatives. This is a grueling process, but its successes include location of the genes for muscular dystrophy, cystic fibrosis, and Huntington's disease, the condition that killed folk singer Woody Guthrie.

This kind of mapping requires a set of markers, which are simply identifiable physical locations on a chromosome.

One goal gene mappers have achieved is to identify a set of markers regularly spaced at close intervals throughout all of the human chromosomes.

Genetic maps have thus far been used to seek out single genes responsible for inherited disorders. This effort relies on molecular patterns, or markers, in chromosomes that are inherited along with a gene that causes an inherited disorder. One of the early goals of the Human Genome Project was to develop dense maps of markers, spaced evenly through the genome. That goal was reached by 1994, when an international group of scientists published a map containing nearly 6,000 markers, spaced less than 1 million base pairs apart. Genes can now be mapped in a matter of months or less.

Another method is to make a physical map that gives the actual structure of the DNA. Such a map is made by chopping a chromosome into many pieces, which will have overlapping ends. By identifying the overlapping ends in a set of pieces, it is possible to put the pieces into an ordered sequence. Physical maps come in varying scales, depending on the size of the pieces in a given map.

In 1990, the Human Genome Project adopted something called a sequence-tagged site (STS) as the basic unit of a physical map. An STS is a sequence of bases that is unique in a genome. The goal of the Human Genome Project is to produce STS markers spaced at intervals of approximately 100,000 base pairs on every chromosome, for a total of 30,000 STSs in all. By the mid-1990s, genome scientists had placed more than 15,000 STSs on their physical map and the goal of 30,000 was in sight.

Gene hunters will use STSs as mileposts to tell them how close they are to the gene they are seeking. Before physical mapping began, such a hunt could take years, but now it can be done in months or even weeks. And because some STSs come from markers on the genetic linkage map, the markers will connect information from the two kinds of maps.

When Jim Watson became the director of the Human Genome Project, he placed himself at the center of several controversies, scientific and otherwise. Scientifically, there were fears that the project could destroy the intimate, personal feel that prevailed then in biological research, diverting money from small, productive research efforts into a giant federal bureaucracy that would have little impact. And medically there were fears that the discovery of the genes responsible for many human illnesses could lead to a program of eugenics, in which humans carrying disease-causing genes could be subjected to mandatory treatments—whether they wanted them or not.

Soon after he became head of the genome project, Watson answered the first criticism by saying that the project was "a way of actually focusing medical research. . . . American biomedical research is in a crisis generated by its own success. There are too many good things to do. . . . I think many major diseases will be understood when we can get their genetic basis."

Watson dealt with the second, medical ethics, controversy by declaring that 3 percent of the genome project's budget would be devoted to study and research on the ethical implications of mapping the human genome. Over 15 years, that could amount to almost $90 million, by far the largest amount of money ever targeted to fund biomedical ethics studies. He also created an ethics committee made up of individuals known to be critics of the misuse of genetic information.

This commitment of government money to the study of ethical issues in the genome program was unprecedented. So was Watson's stand in making bioethics an integral part of a government biological research program. Many biologists disagreed with Watson's approach, but he was steadfast in defending it.

In an interview, Watson noted that "we have to be aware of the really terrible past of eugenics, where incomplete knowledge was used in a cavalier and rather awful way, both in the United States and in Germany. We have to reassure people that their own DNA is private and that no one else can get at it. We're going to have to pass laws to reassure them. But we don't want people rushing and passing laws without a lot of serious discussion first."

Watson's stand on ethical issues became one of his lasting contributions to the genome project. In the 1990s, the NIH's National Center for Human Genome Research devoted 5 percent of its yearly budget, even more than Watson had allocated, to the study of the ethical, legal, and social implications (ELSI) of genome research. The Department of Energy also committed money for the purpose.

In the late 1990s, ELSI established four high-priority areas. One was the use and interpretation of genetic information, which focused on the effect of new genetic information on health insurance—for example, on whether health insurance companies should be forbidden to deny coverage to a woman who carries a gene known to be related to breast cancer. "Insurance providers should be prohibited from using genetic information . . . to deny or limit any coverage," an ELSI committee recommended.

A second effort concentrated on the application of new genetic knowledge to ordinary health care. Committees were established to lay out principles for the use of genetic tests, to recommend the best ways of treating individuals who wanted to be tested for the gene alteration that causes cystic fibrosis, and to conduct several studies on the issues surrounding DNA testing and counseling with regard to the risk of breast, ovarian, and colon cancer. Guidelines for informing individuals about the benefits and possible risks of genetic testing were also established. And finally, the project supported programs to inform the public at large about genetic technologies and their medical uses.

Watson won praise not only for his emphasis on ethical considerations but also for being a good manager. Under his leadership, the budget for the genome project rose to $160 million a year at a time when there was great pressure to hold down the overall federal budget. One medical journal commented that "it is generally agreed that the indispensable, magic ingredient was Watson's charm, drive and dazzlement of our scientifically illiterate Congress—which easily warmed to the renowned author of *The Double Helix.*"

Everything changed dramatically, however, when James Wyngaarden was replaced as head of the National Institutes of Health by a new director, Bernadine Healy, in 1991. Healy and Watson just did not get along. Their first public disagreement had taken place back in 1985, before the beginning of the Human Genome Project, when Ronald Reagan was President. Healy was then Deputy Director for Biomedical Affairs in the Office of Science and Technology Policy. At one point Watson complained publicly about the Reagan administration's attitude toward genetics, saying that "the person in charge of biology is either a woman or unimportant. They had to put a woman someplace."

Healy took this observation personally. She already had experienced sexism in the medical community when she had been one of just 10 female students in her class at Harvard Medical School. She bluntly called Watson's statement "an offense to both men and women." Watson did not apologize, saying he was criticizing the administration, not Healy. This occasion proved to be just the first of many arguments that took place when Healy moved into her new position as Watson's boss. First Healy expressed concern about Watson's holding his government post while he was still head of a private laboratory, and the fact that he was only a part-time administrator for the project. Then Watson criticized a decision made by Healy to take out government patents on thousands of DNA sequences identified by NIH researchers.

This decision split the biomedical community. Some scientists said that patents were necessary to ensure that new genetic discoveries would be put to use promptly. Others argued that patents violated the traditional belief that scientific discoveries should be made available without restriction. Watson and Healy were on diametrically opposite sides of the dispute. Healy said patents were necessary to protect the government's interests. Watson called the decision "lunacy" and said it would impede research. Healy then charged that Watson was "excessively profane and vulgar." It became obvious that something had to give.

A final confrontation was put off for a while when Watson met with Healy in 1991 and agreed to stop making public statements about the patent issue. In private, however, he continued to attack her. Inevitably, word got back to her about the verbal attacks. Their disagreements grew even more intense when scientists throughout the world criticized a decision by the U.S. government to take out foreign, as well as American, patents on Humane Genome Project discoveries. Watson wanted to hold an international meeting to discuss the issue, but Healy ordered him not to.

The showdown came through a dispute with Frederick Bourke, a businessman who wanted to set up a commercial genetic mapping company. He was luring away scientists in England and the United States who were doing genetic sequencing work. Watson began to fight that effort, and he ultimately succeeded in doing so. But it was the beginning of the end for his tenure at the Human Genome Project.

Bourke complained to Healy, as did other scientists who had been involved in Bourke's effort. Specifically, Bourke said that Watson had been consulting with other biotechnology companies about a commercial program of his own. Bourke also complained that Watson had been excessively insulting when he heard that Bourke was trying to lure government genome researchers into a commercial venture. That accusation made Healy start an inquiry into Watson's financial holdings.

The review showed that Watson owned stock in biotechnology companies that conceivably could benefit from the genome project. Although the investigators said there was no conflict of interest in Watson's holdings, Healy refused to sign a waiver saying that nothing was wrong.

The Watson–Healy confrontations continued. At one congressional hearing, Watson said, "I think it would be better if we did not patent sequences that you don't understand." Healy said that until some issues were resolved, "NIH is taking a protective posture." The next day, Watson told some close friends that he would resign as director of the genome project. He handed in his resignation on April 10, 1992. "I would say that this is the lowest moment of my life—to work so hard and be so badly treated," he told a newspaper reporter.

Watson returned to Cold Spring Harbor, where he has continued his valuable research and training of new scientists. The work of the genome project goes on, in many laboratories. Sequencing is done by machine, using either a technology invented by Frederick Sanger of Cambridge University or one developed by Walter Gilbert of Harvard University. The use of advanced technology is one reason why there are great hopes for achieving the year 2005 target date for completing the Human Genome Project.

The story of James Watson and Francis Crick is still being told. Their achievements as teachers and researchers continue to mount. The science of molecular biology, which they did so much to help create, continues to grow explosively. Yet nothing can dim the luster of what they did decades ago.

While their later careers have been full of successes and honors, Watson and Crick will be known forever for what they achieved in their three years of work together at Cambridge University: They discovered the secret of life.

I n February 1997, two teams of biologists reported that they had succeeded in cloning mammals, an achievement that aroused fears that biological technology could lead to genetic copying of human beings.

A clone is a genetically identical copy of a living creature. While some researchers had previously produced genetically identical animals by dividing embryos soon after they were formed by the union of a sperm cell and an egg cell, many biologists had said it might never be possible to clone an organism as complex as a mammal. The problem, they said, was that the DNA of an adult cell becomes differentiated into specialized cells like skin cells and eye cells. That differentiation, they said, means that some genes are

The world's first clone of an adult animal is a sheep named D here in her pen at the Roslin Institute in Edinburgh, Scotland.

"turned off" permanently, so that cells from an adult would be unable to form a complete new organism.

A group led by Dr. Ian Wilmut at the Roslin Institute in Edinburgh, Scotland, was the first to report an experiment that proved the doubters to be wrong. His report was quickly followed by a disclosure that scientists in Oregon had cloned two rhesus monkeys, a species more closely related to humans than are sheep.

Wilmut first removed a cell from the mammary gland of an adult sheep. Then he deprived that cell of nutrients, thus freezing its DNA reproductive cycle. Next he took an egg cell from another adult sheep and removed its DNA-containing nucleus. The two cells were then fused so that the DNA of the egg cell was replaced by the DNA from the adult cell. The altered egg cell, carrying the DNA from the adult sheep, began to divide and form an embryo. It was then implanted in the womb of another ewe, where it multiplied to become a female lamb that was born normally. Tests showed that the DNA of this lamb, named Dolly, was identical with that of the sheep that had donated the DNA.

The process that resulted in the production of the clone was not very efficient. Dr. Wilmut actually fused 227 mammary cells with the same number of eggs, but only 29 of those eggs developed into embryos. When the embryos were implanted in sheep, only 13 became pregnant, and only one carried the pregnancy to a successful end. Yet even these small numbers mark the beginning of a new era in biological science.

There are several possible uses for cloning in industry, medicine, and agriculture. "What this will mostly be used for is to produce health care products," Dr. Wilmut said. "It will enable us to study genetic diseases for which there is presently no cure and track down the mechanisms that are involved."

In health care, clones could be made of cells, to produce pharmaceutical products. Scientists would clone animals that were genetically engineered to make medically useful proteins, which would then be secreted in their milk. Cloning could be used to make exact copies of animals that are especially good at producing milk, wool, or meat. It could also be used to develop animal organs that could be transplanted into human recipients—something that is not possible now because of the genetic differences between animals and humans.

As for human cloning, it is banned by law in Great Britain and a number of other countries, but not in the United States. Any attempt to clone a human being anywhere would create major legal and ethical questions. But it is still possible that some scientist somewhere in this country will sooner or later try this ultimate experiment.

CHRONOLOGY

1916
Francis Harry Compton Crick is born in Northampton, England

1928
James Dewey Watson is born in Chicago, Illinois

1940
Crick's studies interrupted by war; he joins the Admiralty

1944
Oswald Avery identifies DNA as the material in genes

1946
Watson receives undergraduate degree in biology from University of Chicago

1947
Crick joins Strangeways Laboratory at Cambridge University

1950
Watson receives Ph.D. from Indiana University

1950
Maurice Wilkins receives first X-ray diffraction images of DNA

1951
Watson and Crick meet at the Cavendish Laboratory of Cambridge University

1951
Linus Pauling describes protein's structure as an alpha helix

1952
Alfred Hershey and Martha Chase show that DNA is the genetic material of viruses

1953
Watson and Crick publish their first papers on DNA

1953

Linus Pauling describes the wrong triple-helix structure for DNA

1953

Watson and Crick publish a paper giving the correct structure of DNA

1953

Watson and Crick publish follow-up papers on DNA

1961

Watson becomes a professor at Harvard University

1962

Watson, Crick, and Wilkins receive Nobel Prize for Medicine.

1976

Crick goes to the Salk Institute for Biological Studies in La Jolla, California, as nonresident fellow

1976

Watson becomes director of Cold Spring Harbor Laboratory on Long Island, New York

1977

Crick joins Salk Institute permanently

1981

Crick publishes book on theory of directed panspermia

1988

Watson appointed associate director of the Human Genome Research office at the National Institutes of Health

1989

Watson appointed director of the Human Genome Project

1992

Watson leaves the Human Genome Project to return to Cold Spring Harbor Laboratory

1994

Watson becomes president of Cold Spring Harbor Laboratory

FURTHER READING

Bishop, Jerry E., and Michael Waldholz. *Genome*. New York: Simon & Schuster, 1990.

Cook-Deegan, Robert. *The Gene Wars*. New York: Norton, 1994.

Crick, Francis. *The Astonishing Hypothesis: The Scientific Search for the Soul*. New York: Scribner, 1994.

Crick, Francis. *Life Itself: Its Origin and Nature*. New York: Simon & Schuster, 1981.

Crick, Francis. *What Mad Pursuit: A Personal View of Scientific Discovery*. New York: Basic Books, 1988.

Fried, John J. *The Mystery of Heredity*. New York: John Day, 1971.

Hilton, Bruce, Daniel Callahan, Maureen Harris, and Peter Condliffe. *Ethical Issues in Human Genetics: Genetic Counseling and the Use of Genetic Knowledge*. New York: Plenum Press, 1973.

Hood, Leroy, and Daniel J. Kevles. *The Case of Codes*. Cambridge: Harvard University Press, 1992.

Judson, Horace Freeland. *The Eighth Day of Creation*. New York: Simon & Schuster, 1979.

McKusick, V. A. *Human Genetics*. Englewood Cliffs, NJ: Prentice-Hall, 1969.

Newton, David E. *James Watson & Francis Crick: Discovery of the Double Helix and Beyond*. New York: Facts on File, 1992.

Nyhan, William. *The Heredity Factor*. New York: Grosset and Dunlap, 1976.

Pines, Maya. *Mapping the Human Genome*. Bethesda, MD: Howard Hughes Medical Institute, 1987.

Shapiro, R. *The Human Blueprint: The Race to Unlock the Secrets of Our Genetic Script*. New York: St. Martin's Press, 1991.

U.S. Department of Health and Human Services. *The Human Genome Project: From Maps to Medicine*. Springfield, VA: National Technical Information Service, 1995.

U.S. Department of Health and Human Services. *Understanding Our Genetic Inheritance: The U.S. Genome Project, The First Five Years*. Springfield, VA: National Technical Information Service, 1990.

U.S. Congress Office of Technology Assessment. *Mapping Our Genes: Genome Projects—How Big? How Fast?* Baltimore, MD: Johns Hopkins University Press, 1988.

Watson, Elizabeth L. *Houses for Science: A Pictorial History of Cold Spring Harbor Laboratory*. Plainview, NY: Cold Spring Harbor Laboratory Press, 1991.

Watson, James D. *The DNA Story: A Documentary History of Gene Cloning*. San Francisco: Freeman, 1981.

Watson, James D. *The Double Helix: A Personal Account of the Discovery of the Structure of DNA*. New York: Atheneum, 1968.

Watson, James D., et al. *Molecular Biology of the Gene*. 4th ed. Menlo Park, CA: Benjamin/Cummings, 1988.

Watson, James D., Michael Gilman, Jan Witkowski, and Mark Zoller. *Recombinant DNA*. 2nd ed. New York: Scientific American Books, 1992.

Wills, Christopher. *Exons, Introns and Talking Genes*. New York: Basic Books, 1991.

PICTURE CREDITS

Edward Edelson is a free-lance science writer in New York City. The author of 19 books on science, including two college chemisty textbooks and several young adult books, he was the science editor for the *New York Daily News* from 1971 to 1991 and an editor and writer for *Family Health* magazine from 1969 to 1971. He served as president of the National Association of Science Writers from 1979 to 1980 and has received numerous honors for his writing from groups such as the American Dental Association, the American Medical Association, the American Institute of Physics, and the American Cancer Society. He holds a B.S. in journalism from New York University and attended the Columbia School of Journalism Advanced Science Writing Program.

Owen Gingerich is Professor of Astronomy and of the History of Science at the Harvard-Smithsonian Center for Astrophysics in Cambridge, Massachusetts. The author of more than 400 articles and reviews, he has also written *The Great Copernicus Chase and Other Adventures in Astronomical History* and *The Eye of Heaven: Ptolemy, Copernicus, Kepler.*